Finanzwirtschaft, Banken und Bankmanagement | Finance, Banks and Bank Management

Reihe herausgegeben von
Axel Wieandt, Königstein, Deutschland
Sebastian C. Moenninghoff, Vallendar, Deutschland

Die Reihe präsentiert Forschungsbeiträge aus den Bereichen Finanzwirtschaft, Banken und Bankmanagement, die sich durch hohe wissenschaftliche Qualität und Praxisbezug auszeichnen. Sie richtet sich an Akademiker und Praktiker.

The series presents research from the fields of finance, banking and bank management, which are characterized by high scientific quality and practical relevance. It is aimed at academics and practitioners.

More information about this series at http://www.springer.com/series/16023

Gevorg Hunanyan

The Consequences of Short-Sale Constraints on the Stability of Financial Markets

With a foreword by Hon.-Prof. Dr. Axel Wieandt and Dr. Sebastian Moenninghoff

Springer Gabler

Gevorg Hunanyan
Technical University Kaiserslautern
Kaiserslautern, Germany

Dissertation Technische Universität Kaiserslautern, Germany, 2019

D 386

ISSN 2524-6429 ISSN 2524-6437 (electronic)
Finanzwirtschaft, Banken und Bankmanagement | Finance, Banks and Bank Management
ISBN 978-3-658-27955-4 ISBN 978-3-658-27956-1 (eBook)
https://doi.org/10.1007/978-3-658-27956-1

Springer Gabler

This Springer Gabler imprint is published by the registered company Springer Fachmedien Wiesbaden GmbH part of Springer Nature.
The registered company address is: Abraham-Lincoln-Str. 46, 65189 Wiesbaden, Germany

To Lia

Foreword

Gevorg Hunanyan's thesis examines how restrictions on short-selling of securities impact investor behavior, market prices and financial stability. The analysis is based on extensions of the standard Capital Asset Pricing Model including a dynamic model framework to analyze long-run price implications of short-selling restrictions. From a microeconomic perspective, the thesis finds that the individual investor default probability depends on investors' risk preferences and that restrictions on short-selling can increase the individual investor default risk. From a macroeconomic perspective, the analysis shows that short sale restrictions can impact prices both upwards and downwards, depending on subjective investor beliefs. From a financial stability point of view, Mr. Hunanyan's thesis finds that short sale restrictions potentially decrease systematic risk, while a prohibition of short-selling increases systematic risk. The impact of short-selling on financial markets and financial stability has been frequently discussed during times of financial crises. Banks have lobbied for restrictions on short-selling, blaming short sellers to aggravate a vicious cycle of stock price decline and vanishing trust from counterparties and customers. In contrast, hedge funds have argued that restrictions on short-selling distort the market mechanism and artificially inflate share prices. Hedge funds further claimed that short-selling prohibitions limit investors' ability to hedge investment risk during banks' rights issues, which would potentially increase banks' cost of capital in times they are in need of new funds to strengthen their balance sheets. Similarly, short-selling has been used by investors to partially hedge exposure from investing in banks' contingent convertible bonds, an important tool for banks to strengthen their capital in times of distress. Further, financial institutions not covered by short-selling restrictions have argued that any asymmetric restrictions on short-selling might put overproportionate pressure on their own share prices since investors would seek similar exposure by short selling correlated stocks, pointing to the inevitable risk of unintended consequences of regulations.

With trust being an essential component for the functioning of a fractional reserve financial system, regulators are concerned about the impact sharp stock price declines may have on financial institutions' ability to access funding that is required to support their business. To the extent creditors and depositors of a bank link a sharply falling stock price to an increased likelihood of losses the bank may incur, they will require a higher risk premium or withdraw funds. The opaqueness of banks' assets and the close interaction of the overall economic development with banks' potential credit losses make banks vulnerable to severe funding constraints or even bank runs. In this context, short selling as a contributor to liquidity crises would increase the probability of default of banks, and, from a government exposure perspective, result in an increased government exposure at distress to the financial system, implying higher potential losses from implicit or explicit government guarantees to the financial system.

Regulatory measures to limit short selling range from disclosure requirements for short positions to restrictions and (temporary) bans of short selling for certain financial securities. For example, in September 2008, at the height of the financial crisis, the U.S. and European financial regulators introduced temporary bans on short-selling. The UK Financial Services Authority instituted a short-selling ban for 32 UK financial institutions in September 2008, which was matched by the SEC with a temporary ban on all short sales in 799 financial stocks. Likewise, the German regulator BaFin banned the short-selling of the stocks of 11 financial firms. An evaluation of regulatory measures from a government's risk-return perspective takes into account the implications for both economic growth and financial stability.[1] From an economic growth perspective, short-selling restrictions or bans, especially if temporary, appear to have less of a direct impact on long-term growth as do other more profound measures such as for example a substantial increase in regulatory capital requirements for banks. However, from a risk or economic volatility perspective, a direct interference in stock market prices should be carefully evaluated, including aspects around implementation efficiency - i.e. the certainty of achieving the desired effect of a regulatory intervention. This is where Gevorg Hunanyan's thesis provides an important contribution by furthering the understanding of short-selling, also in a dynamic model context. The finding that different regulatory designs of limiting short-selling - restrictions versus prohibitions - can lead to significantly different outcomes illustrates the necessity to carefully calibrate regulations in this area to achieve the desired effect.

Axel Wieandt

Sebastian Moenninghoff

[1] Compare Moenninghoff, Sebastian C. (2018): The Regulation of Systemically Relevant Banks, Springer Gabler, 2018.

Acknowledgements

First of all I would like to express my sincere gratitude to my advisor Prof. Jan Wenzelburger for his constant support and his fruitful and passionate discussions. Throughout the years I could always rely on his support. I would also like to thank my co-supervisor Prof. Philipp Weinschenk for his constructive suggestions during our seminars.

I greatly benefited from the working atmosphere at our research group. I am thankful to my colleagues Dr. Conrad Spanaus, Theresia Seltmann, Helena Krebs, Dr. Rebecca Schmitt and Dr. Oscar Nieto. Special thanks go to Conrad Spanaus for his constant readiness for discussions, many helpful suggestions and the proofreading of the manuscript. Likewise, I am grateful to Nico Schilling for stimulating discussions and his support with the implementation of the model.

Furthermore, I would like to take this opportunity to thank Springer Gabler, in particular Mrs. Carina Reibold and Mrs. Anita Wilke for their kind support. Also many thanks to Prof. Axel Wieandt and Dr. Sebastian Moenninghoff for their helpful comments on the manuscript.

Last but not least, I would like to thank my family for their support during my pursuit of a Ph.D degree. I thank my parents and my brother for their willingness to support me in any decision I made. Moreover, I would like to express my gratitude to my wife, Mane Harutyunyan, for her patience and tolerance over the last years. Special thanks go to my parents-in-law and my sister-in-law who helped me with their care. I am thankful to my little daughter, Lia, for her patience and her forgiveness of my absence during the writing of the thesis.

Gevorg Hunanyan

Contents

List of Figures and Tables

Abstract

The aim of this thesis is to study the consequences of short-sale constraints on the stability of security markets. After the financial crisis of 2008, short-selling - borrowing and selling a financial instrument with the obligation to buy back the stock in the future - has been heavily criticised by regulators and the media. Theoretical contributions conclude that restricting short-sales will lead to overpriced securities and thus prevent a market decline. These approaches, however, consider a single-asset financial market with partially heterogeneous investors only. Applying a more general framework with *fully heterogeneous* investors who participate in a financial market with *many assets*, this thesis establishes results which do not support this view.

The objective of this thesis is threefold. Firstly, to study the consequences of short-sale constraints on the investor's portfolio selection, risk-taking behaviour as well as default probability. Secondly, to formulate a market structure and determine the impact of constrained short-selling on equilibrium asset prices. Finally, to analyse the effect of short-sale constraints on the *systematic risk* of the financial market.

For an individual investor, we show that the effectiveness of short-sale constraints in reducing portfolio risk as well as default risk depends on the investor's risk preferences. On the financial market, short-sale constraints may distort equilibrium prices upwards as well as downwards. The direction of the price distortion solely depends on the investors' subjective second moment beliefs regarding future gross returns. Under a wide dispersion of second moment beliefs, short-sale constraints may amplify a market decline rather than stabilise the financial market. Finally, we introduce a modification of the security market line for financial markets in which short-sale constraints are enacted. This time-dependent security market line allows to decompose the risk measure standard deviation into systematic and non-systematic risk. We show that a restricted short-sale constraint potentially decreases the systematic risk, while a prohibition on short-sales increases it.

Introduction

The Dutch East India Company (Vereenigde Oostindische Compagni or VOC) was a multinational corporation founded on March 20, 1602 by Dutch merchants. In 1607, the largest shareholder of the company, Isaac Le Maire, was invited by the French King Henry IV to advise on the establishment of a French-chartered trading company. By 1609, the VOC was still paying no dividend. Anticipating the establishment of the French overseas company, Le Maire sold all his shares and *sold short* additional shares, i.e. he borrowed and sold unowned shares. He speculated on a price decline so that he could repurchase the borrowed shares at a lower price and return to the owners in the future. Over the next twelve months the share of VOC dropped by 12%. In January of 1610 the first short-sale constraint, the world has seen, was enacted.

Short-sellers like Le Maire have been blamed for the majority of financial crises in the 400 years since this Dutch episode. In 1720, shortly after the stock markets became established, a financial bubble broke out in England and France. The market collapse in France was caused by speculation in shares of the Mississippi Company: within 6 months the share price rose from 500 livres to 10.000 livres and dropped back to 500 livres (see e.g. GREGORIOU (2011)). Meanwhile, similar dramatic fluctuations in the share price of the South Sea Company occurred in England. In both countries short-sellers, who profited from the decline, were fined and short-sales prohibited (CHANCELLOR (2001)). Unlike Le Maire, who used *insider information* and caused the decline, there was no evidence of market manipulation in the crises of 1720. The *motive* of short-selling, however, was the same: to make profits from a decline in the share price.

Financial textbooks (see e.g. LEVY AND SARNAT (1994) and ASNESS (2004)) distinguish between *profitability* and *diversification motive* of short-selling. The profitability motive explains the notion of a short-sale as the counterpart of a "long-sale", i.e. buying the security with the expectations that the asset will rise in value. However, short-selling is generally viewed as more risky than long-selling as prices can always rise, yielding the possibility of unlimited losses for a short position. In some textbooks the profitability motive is

G. Hunanyan, *The Consequences of Short-Sale Constraints on the Stability of Financial Markets*, Finanzwirtschaft, Banken und Bankmanagement | Finance, Banks and Bank Management, https://doi.org/10.1007/978-3-658-27956-1_1

better known as the *speculation motive*. Modern portfolio theory concludes that *efficient portfolios* are "best" in the sense that they provide the smallest portfolio risk for a prescribed level of return or the highest average return for a prescribed level of risk. These portfolios are also known as *optimally diversified* portfolios. Investors seek to reduce portfolio risk through an optimal diversification. To this aim they take short and long positions in a variety of risky assets. Consequently, limiting short-sales might reduce diversification possibilities and increase *non-diversifiable* risk.

Proponents of a frictionless market therefore argue that short-selling allows investors to hold well-diversified portfolios, leading to smaller portfolio risk. Moreover, they claim that short-selling improves market efficiency as it reflects the views of all investors, both optimists and pessimists. Along this lines, in front of the Committee on Rules of the U.S. House of Representatives in 1917, the financier Bernard Baruch stated:

> "To enjoy the advantages of a free market, one must have both buyers and sellers, both bulls (long-sellers) and bears (short-sellers). A market without bears would be like a nation without a free press. There would be no one to criticise and restrain the false optimism that always leads to disaster."

On the other hand, opponents of a frictionless market argue that short-sellers can amplify or even cause a market decline by placing a downward pressure on the market. In their view, there should be short-sale constraints in place to avoid a precipitous downward spiral of asset prices. A worth-noting study of Misra et al. (2011) supports this view. The authors find evidence that, not long after the Securities and Exchange Commission (SEC) repealed the "uptick rule" (a short-selling regulation) on July 6, 2007, Citigroup's stock experienced an unusual increase in trading volume and decrease in price. This market manipulation reinforced the claim that relaxing the regulation was an integral part of Lehman Brothers' bankruptcy on September 15, 2008. Following this council, regulators around the world, including the Securities and Exchange Commission in the US, the Financial Services Authority (FSA) in the United Kingdom and Federal Financial Supervisory Authority (BaFin) in Germany, restricted or even prohibited short-sales of particular stocks. BaFin, for example, announced the prohibition on short-selling of 11 German financial stocks from the insurance and banking industry. SEC went one step further and banned short-sales of 799 financial stocks for 14 trading days from September 19th through October 8th of 2008. Two years later, SEC established the permanent "alternative uptick rule" (formally known as Rule 201), which disallows investors to short-sale if the price of the asset has dropped more than 10 percent in one day.

The effectiveness of short-sale constraints in stabilising the financial market, however, has been questionable from a political as well as an academic point of view. A variety of scientific contributions explore different aspects of market stability and short-sale constraints.

Assuming heterogeneous beliefs on the return distribution, Nakata (2013) analyses welfare effects of short-sale constraints. The empirical contributions by Haruvy and Noussair (2006) and Xiong (2013) study the effect of short-sales on both, the incidence and magnitude of market bubbles.

Figlewski and Webb (1993) examine the relation between short-sales and options trading. The impact of short-sale constraints on liquidity (Liu and Wang (2018)), stock price volatility (Chang et al. (2006)), and trading volume (Zhang (1997)) is investigated as well. Another strand of financial literature focuses on the consequences of restricted short-selling on the investors' portfolio selection. Levy and Ritov (2011) show that the proportion of short positions in mean-variance efficient portfolios converges to 50% as the number of assets increases. Because closed-form efficient portfolios are difficult to find for economies with short-sale constraints, the portfolio optimisation models Bongini et al. (2002) and Smimou et al. (2008) resort to numerical approximations. Ross (1977), Dybvig (1984), Markowitz (1990) and Alexander (1993) investigate the relation between risk and return of efficient portfolios in the presence of short-sale constraints. Moreover, the impact of constrained borrowing on excess returns is studied empirically in Figlewski (1981) as well as theoretically in Basak and Cuoco (1998), Kogan et al. (2007), and Chabakauri (2013). The contributions of Black (1972) and Won et al. (2008) relax the assumption of unrestricted borrowing of the risk-free bond. While Black (1972) generalises the well-known security market line, Won et al. (2008) establish existence of positive equilibrium asset prices in the mean-variance economy with heterogeneous expectations.

In enacting the short-sale constraint, regulatory authorities sought to eliminate a market decline by preventing a downward movement of asset prices. Therefore, we differentiate our analysis from the above cited strands of literature by examining the effectiveness of short-sale constraints as an instrument to prevent a market decline. There is a comprehensive empirical as well as theoretical literature which restricts attention on the relationship between short-sale constraints and stock prices. Whereas empirical studies (e.g. Choie and Hwang (1994), Boehme et al. (2006), Nagel (2005), Bris et al. (2007) and Jones and Lamont (2002)) as well as laboratory experiments (e.g. Fellner and Theissen (2014)) indicate that asset prices are higher with short-sale constraints, theoretical contributions show inconclusive results. The modern asset pricing theory has its origin in the Capital Asset Pricing Model (CAPM) developed by Sharpe (1964), Lintner (1965), and Mossin (1966). It deals with the central aspects of capital markets equilibria and is built on the foundations of the portfolio theory initiated by MARKOWITZ (1952) and TOBIN (1958). In its original form, the CAPM is static and considers investors with homogeneous beliefs as portfolio managers who maximise expected utility. In this framework, SHARPE (1964), LINTNER (1969) and ROSS (1977) show that short-sale constraints are non-binding, as each investor holds a proportion of the total supply of all risky securities, the market portfolio. The market portfolio is then efficient and the traditional form of the CAPM holds.

However, in a world of uncertainty, it is more natural to assume that beliefs are heterogeneous. Considering a *single-asset* financial market in which heterogeneous investors interact, MILLER (1977) and HARRISON AND KREPS (1978), conclude that the equilibrium asset price is distorted upwards whenever short-sale constraints are enacted. The authors claim that the presence of short-sale constraints increases the aggregate demand as restrictions on short-sales expel the pessimistic investors and reflect merely the view of optimists who expect the asset price to increase. Considering a *multi-asset* financial market, JARROW (1980) contradicts this *overpricing theory* by means of a counterexample. The author shows that equilibrium asset prices may decline due to a so-called *substitution effect*. Other notable works contradicting the overpricing hypothesis are given by DIAMOND AND VERRECCHIA (1987) and GALLMEYER AND HOLLIFIELD (2008). The latter authors find that imposing the constraint reduces the stock price if and only if the optimistic investors' intertemporal elasticity of substitution is less than one. DIAMOND AND VERRECCHIA (1987), on the other hand, argue that the fully rational and risk-neutral market maker takes the existence of short-sale constraints into account and sets bid and ask prices at the correct level. In the long term overpricing will thus not occur.

Summarising, it seems that constrained short-selling can distort equilibrium prices upwards as well as downwards if the financial market consists of multiple assets. However, a comprehensive theoretical framework which establishes conditions on the effectiveness of short-sale constraints in stabilising the financial market, by preventing a downward movement of asset prices, is still missing.

The aim of this thesis is therefore to develop a theoretical framework that complements the existing approaches by answering, among others, the following questions:

- How do short-sale constraints affect the investor's portfolio selection, risk-taking behaviour and default probability?
- What are the consequences of short-sale constraints on equilibrium asset prices?

- Is it possible to study the effect of short-sale constraints on the systematic risk of the financial market?

This thesis is divided into four chapters. The *first chapter* covers the static framework of our model. Special emphasis is placed on the investor's decision making in the presence of short-sale constraints. We consider an investor with mean-variance preferences who seeks to maximise utility by choosing an optimal portfolio which satisfies the short-sale constraint. In Section 1.2 we establish existence and uniqueness of the utility-maximising portfolio by generalising the classical two-fund separation theorem, first developed by TOBIN (1958) and LINTNER (1965), to the case of constrained short-selling. The classical result that optimal portfolios are mean-variance efficient, in the sense that they provide the smallest portfolio risk for a prescribed level of return or the highest average return for a prescribed level of risk, will be extended to the case of constrained short-selling. It will be shown that the multivariate portfolio decision problem reduces to a univariate problem of finding optimal portfolio risk σ. In Section 1.3, we then study the consequences of short-sale constraints on the investor's *risk-taking behaviour*. It is intuitively clear that short-sale constraints typically restrict the set of profitable investment opportunities and may therefore adversely affect the default risk of investors. For elliptically distributed returns, we show in Section 1.4 that the effectiveness of short-sale constraints in reducing the default risk depends on the investor's risk preferences.

Chapter 2 formulates the market structure and studies the consequences of constrained short-selling on equilibrium asset prices. There, we establish the central results of this thesis. In Section 2.1 we prove existence and uniqueness of an asset market equilibrium in the presence of short-sale constraints. For the case with two investors, Section 2.2 establishes an explicit market clearing price formula allowing to determine the conditions of overpricing. It turns out that the subjective second moments alone determine the direction of how short-sale constraints distort equilibrium asset prices. In particular, we show that constrained short-selling achieves the desired effect of overpricing whenever the subjective covariance matrices differ by a positive factor. In Section 2.3 we study the case of three and more investors and show that the form of equilibrium asset prices cannot be determined without use of an algorithmic procedure.

Building upon the static framework, the *third chapter* embeds the model into the theory of deterministic dynamical systems in a random environment. Following WENZELBURGER (2009), this is achieved by first reinterpreting the static equilibrium map as a *temporary equilibrium* map and second, allowing investors to re-evaluate their expectations by an adaptive forecasting rule.

From this perspective, Chapter 3 is concerned with the impact of short-sale constraints on the long-run behaviour of equilibrium asset prices and allocations. In Section 3.1 we formulate the market structure in which two *chartists* interact. Chartist are modelled as trend chaser who apply weighted average of past asset prices to predict future stock prices. Moreover, we suppose that in each period a group of noise traders, whose portfolio decisions are not captured by standard microeconomic decision models, participate in the financial market. The numerical simulation study, presented in Section 3.2, indicates that noise traders' random transactions as well as a wide dispersion of covariance matrices, may distort equilibrium asset prices downwards. As a further research question, Section 3.3 examines the consequences of short-sale constraints on the volatility of the asset price process.

The starting point of the *final chapter* is a more general setting in which, instead of a price evolution generated by agents' characteristics, asset returns are stipulated by an exogenously given stochastic process. In this setting we examine the consequences of short-sale constraints on the "systematic risk" - the amount of risk which cannot be reduced through diversification - of the economy. Assuming that utility-maximising investors have homogeneous expectations and can lend and borrow unlimited amounts under the risk-free rate of interest r_f, the classical CAPM of SHARPE (1964), LINTNER (1965), and MOSSIN (1966) concludes that the relation between expected return and systematic risk is linear. Denoting $\mathbb{E}[r^i]$ and $\mathbb{E}[R_{\mathrm{m}}]$ as the expected return on asset i and the market portfolio, respectively, this relation is given by the *security market line*

$$\mathbb{E}[r^i] = r_f + \beta_{\mathrm{m}}^{(i)}[\mathbb{E}[R_{\mathrm{m}}] - r_f], \tag{SML}$$

where $\beta_{\mathrm{m}}^{(i)}$ is the measure of systematic risk. The market return R_{m} is defined as the sum of all investment returns in the economy. Discarding the above listed assumptions, ROLL (1977) and ROSS (1977) independently show that the SML continues to hold if and only if the market portfolio is efficient. In order to verify the CAPM, empirical studies use a proxy such as S&P 500 or DAX 100 rather than the market portfolio. Since in general these market proxies are inefficient, the security market line and thus the value of the huge amount of empirical research is questionable. To approach this problem, WENZELBURGER (2018B) introduces a *modified market portfolio*, which unlike the standard market portfolio of the CAPM, accounts for diverse and erroneous beliefs of investors and is mean-variance efficient in the sense of MARKOWITZ (1952). For a given exogenous stochastic process of asset returns, the classical security market line is generalised to a time-dependent security market line, allowing a time-dependent dynamic decomposition into systematic and non-systematic risk. Apart from a non-degenerate covariance structure and the possibility of unrestricted short-selling, the paper requires no further assumptions. If, however, short-sales are constrained, this modified market portfolio may become inefficient. In Chapter 4 we therefore aim at the derivation of a time-dependent security market line on the regulated financial market. Since BLACK (1972) already developed a version of CAPM, that relaxes the assumption of unrestricted borrowing of the *riskless* bond, we restrict attention to short-sale constraints on *risky* assets. Section 4.1 studies the consequences of short-sale constraints on the *individual* risk of investors. In particular, we will discuss the hypothesis that short-sale constraints disallow investors to hold well diversified portfolios and increase individual systematic risk. Sections 4.2 and 4.3 will then examine the impact of short-sale constraints on the entire market by re-establishing the security market that allows to decompose risk into systematic and non-systematic risk. For this purpose we replace the modified market portfolio by a mean-variance efficient portfolio which satisfies the enacted short-sale constraint. Conclusions and a comprehensive appendix collecting all technical proofs close this thesis.

1 Portfolio Selection

Following the modelling strategy proposed in the introduction, the present chapter develops the theoretical framework of this thesis. The static model presented here forms the base to analyse the consequences of short-sale constraints on the investor's *portfolio selection* as well as *portfolio risk* and *default risk*.

The present chapter is organised as follows: Section 1.1 introduces our framework and formulates the investor's decision problem. The existence and uniqueness of its solution is established in Section 1.2. In Sections 1.3 and 1.4 the consequences of the short-sale constraint on an investor's risk-taking behaviour as well as default probability are analysed.

1.1 Prerequisites

We extend the Capital Asset Pricing Model (CAPM) developed by SHARPE (1964), LINTNER (1965), and MOSSIN (1966) to incorporate short-sale constraints. The economy considered here is of static nature with dates 0 and 1. On the financial market traders can invest their initial wealth w_0 in a portfolio $(x, y) \in \mathbb{R}^n \times \mathbb{R}$ of $n+1$ assets. In the vector $x = (x^{(1)}, \dots, x^{(n)})^\top \in \mathbb{R}^n$ of n *risky assets*, $x^{(k)}$ denotes the number of shares invested into the k-th risky security. The k-th asset is a liability of the investor and is sold short whenever $x^{(k)} < 0$. The scalar y represents the number of shares invested into the *risk-free* bond which is in perfect elastic supply. The associated price vector of risky assets is denoted by $p = (p^{(1)}, \dots, p^{(n)})^\top \in \mathbb{R}^n$ and the bond price is normalised to one. Assuming that the initial endowment of an investor as well as all prices are denominated in a non-storable consumption good, the investor's budget constraint in period $t = 0$ is given by

$$w_0 = y + \langle p, x \rangle, \tag{1.1}$$

where $\langle \cdot, \cdot \rangle$ denotes the scalar product in $\mathbb{R}^n$. In period $t = 1$, the risk-free bond yields a *deterministic* gross return $R_f = 1 + r_f$ whereas risky assets are

G. Hunanyan, *The Consequences of Short-Sale Constraints on the Stability of Financial Markets*, Finanzwirtschaft, Banken und Bankmanagement | Finance, Banks and Bank Management, https://doi.org/10.1007/978-3-658-27956-1_2

characterised by a *stochastic* pay-off vector $\tilde{q} = (\tilde{q}^{(1)}, \ldots, \tilde{q}^{(n)})^\top$. With this notation, the investor's future wealth becomes

$$\tilde{w}_1 = R_f y + \langle \tilde{q}, x \rangle \overset{(1.1)}{=} R_f w_0 + \langle \tilde{q} - R_f p, x \rangle. \tag{1.2}$$

The uncertainty of $\tilde{w}_1$ is solely determined by the random gross returns $\tilde{q}$. This uncertainty is described by a (subjective) probability distribution $\nu_{\tilde{q}}$ of $\tilde{q}$. It is assumed that the investor does not use the full probability distribution of $\tilde{q}$ but rather its first two moments. Based on $\nu_{\tilde{q}}$, let $\overline{q}^{(k)} := \mathbb{E}[\tilde{q}^{(k)}]$ be the (subjectively) expected gross return of the k-th asset and $V_{ij} := \mathbb{C}\mathrm{ov}[\tilde{q}^{(k)}, \tilde{q}^{(j)}]$ be the (subjective) covariance between the gross returns of the k-th and j-th risky assets. Then, the vector of *expected gross returns* is

$$\overline{q} = (\overline{q}^{(1)}, \ldots, \overline{q}^{(n)})^\top \in \mathbb{R}^n_+,$$

whereas the *covariance matrix* is

$$V = (V_{ij})_{i,j=1,\ldots,n}.$$

For simplicity, we assume that there are no redundant assets, i.e. no asset return can be obtained as a linear combination of the returns of other assets. This assumption is equivalent to require positive definiteness of the symmetric covariance matrix $V \in \mathbb{R}^{n \times n}$. Note that, the formation of the investor's beliefs $(\overline{q}, V)$ is *exogenous*, as in the static framework no re-evaluation of expectations based on past forecasting errors is made. At time $t = 0$ the investor enters the financial market with the beliefs already formed. In the next period prices are realised and the model ends. The extension of the model to an intertemporal one with endogenous expatiations formation is discussed in Chapter 3.

Denoting $\pi = (\pi^{(1)}, \ldots, \pi^{(n)})$ where $\pi^{(k)} := \overline{q}^{(k)} - R_f p^{(k)}$ for all $k = 1, \ldots, n$, as the vector of *expected excess returns*, the expected future wealth and its standard deviation are given by

$$\mathbb{E}[\tilde{w}_1] = R_f w_0 + \langle \pi, x \rangle$$

and

$$\mathbb{V}\mathrm{ar}[\tilde{w}_1]^{\frac{1}{2}} = \langle x, Vx \rangle^{\frac{1}{2}},$$

respectively. The investor's objective function is given by a utility function U that depends solely on the mean and standard deviation of the future wealth. An investor with this mean-variance preferences is formally characterised as follows.

Assumption 1. *An investor is represented by a utility function U depending on the mean μ and the standard deviation σ of future wealth, as well as a probability distribution $\nu_{\tilde{q}}$ over future gross returns, having the following properties:*

1. *The utility function $U : \mathbb{R} \times \mathbb{R}_{+} \to \mathbb{R}$ is continuously differentiable, strictly increasing in μ, strictly decreasing in σ, and strictly quasi-concave.*

2. *The probability distribution $\nu_{\tilde{q}}$ is parametrised by a pair $(\overline{q}, V)$, where $\overline{q}$ is the vector of mean returns and V is the positive definite covariance matrix.*

In essence, Assumption 1 describes the investor as a "standard" consumer in microeconomic theory having preferences over the commodities, *risk* and *return*. Return, measured by the expected future wealth, may be interpreted as a "good", whereas risk, measured by the standard deviation, is a "bad". However, standard deviation as a measure of risk to explain the risk-taking behaviour of agents is criticised in financial literature. Motivated by this, SPANAUS (2018) established an asset pricing model with permitted short-selling in which standard deviation is replaced by a *downside risk measure*. The author was able to generalise many findings of classical portfolio theory to the case with downside risk. In our context with constrained short-selling, to assume that portfolio risk is measured by a more suitable risk measure would be more realistic but at the same time make the model significantly more difficult and much less tractable. However, due to the structural results in SPANAUS (2018), we expect that qualitatively, our results will carry over to the case with downside risk.

Having defined the basic model, we now proceed with introducing the short-sale constraint. Shorting, or a short-sale, is the practice of selling unowned shares and subsequently repurchasing (covering) them. Short-selling is motivated by the view that a security's price will decline, enabling it to be bought back at a lower price to make a profit. The modelling of restrictions on short-sales is widespread in financial literature. ANUFRIEV AND TUINSTRA (2013) introduced an indirect constraint by imposing trading costs for short-selling an asset. DERCOLE AND RADI (2014) modelled the "uptick rule". This regulatory policy is based on "price tests" that allows short-sales only on an uptick, i.e. at a price higher than the last reported one. In classical financial literature[1], short-sale constraints are included by limiting shares to non-negative values. This can be regarded as a full ban on short-sales. In the present thesis, the short-sale constraint is included by restricting the shares to be larger than a prescribed threshold χ. The constraint is merely imposed on one risky as-

[1] see e.g. MILLER (1977), JARROW (1980), MARKOWITZ (1990)

set which, without loss of generality, is assumed to be the n-th asset. More formally, the short-sale restriction is

$$x^{(n)} \geq \chi, \tag{1.3}$$

where $\chi \leq 0$ and $x^{(n)}$ denotes the number of shares invested into the n-th risky asset. The approach suggested in this thesis, thus differs from classical models in two aspects. On the one hand, instead of limiting to the case of a full ban on short-selling, the model allows for a wide range of intermediate setting. On the other hand, the regulation of only one risky asset facilitates the analysis of crossover effects on non-regulated assets. For the short-sale constraint we will distinguish between two cases. If $\chi < 0$ then short-selling of a reasonable size is allowed and we will refer to (1.3) as a "restricted short-sale" constraint. In case that a full ban ($\chi = 0$) on the sale of borrowed shares is established, we will refer to (1.3) as a "prohibited short-sale" constraint.

Setting the expected wealth and the standard deviation associated with a portfolio x as

$$\mathrm{M}(x) := R_f w_0 + \langle \pi, x \rangle$$

and

$$\mathrm{Sd}(x) := \langle x, Vx \rangle^{\frac{1}{2}},$$

respectively, the decision problem of an investor who obeys the short-sale constraint becomes the maximisation problem

$$\max_{x \in X} U(\mathrm{M}(x), \mathrm{Sd}(x)), \tag{1.4}$$

where $X := \{x \in \mathbb{R}^n : x^{(n)} \geq \chi\}$ describes the set of all attainable portfolios. The existence of solutions to (1.4) requires the concept of a *limiting slope* of an indifference curve. Let

$$\mathcal{I}(\mu_0, \sigma_0) := \Big\{(\mu, \sigma) \in \mathbb{R} \times \mathbb{R}_+ \text{ s.t. } U(\mu, \sigma) = U(\mu_0, \sigma_0)\Big\}$$

denote the indifference curve through (μ_0, σ_0). Recall that the slope of any indifference curve in the $\mu - \sigma$ plane is given by the marginal rate of substitution between risk and return,

$$S(\mu, \sigma) := -\frac{\frac{\partial U}{\partial \sigma}(\mu, \sigma)}{\frac{\partial U}{\partial \mu}(\mu, \sigma)}.$$

Following NIELSEN (1988), we will use the marginal rate of substitution S to measure the investor's *risk aversion*. The *limiting slope* of an indifference curve starting in $(\mu_0, 0)$ is then defined by

$$\rho_U(\mu_0) := \sup\Big\{S(\mu, \sigma) : (\mu, \sigma) \in \mathcal{I}(\mu_0, 0)\Big\}.$$

Under the hypotheses of Assumption 1, the unconstrained optimisation problem

$$\max_{x \in \mathbb{R}^n} U(\mathrm{M}(x), \mathrm{Sd}(x)), \tag{1.5}$$

admits a unique maximiser $x^* \in \mathbb{R}^n$, whenever the price of risk[2] is less than the limiting slope $\rho_U(R_f wo)$, see e.g. WENZELBURGER (2010). The solution to (1.5) is given by the Two-fund Separation theorem[3] and is denoted by $x^* = x_{\text{eff}}(\sigma^*)$ where

$$x_{\text{eff}}(\sigma) = \frac{\sigma}{\sqrt{\langle \pi, V^{-1}\pi \rangle}} V^{-1}\pi, \tag{1.6}$$

is the mean-variance efficient portfolio with risk σ, and

$$\sigma^* = \arg\max_{\sigma \geq 0} U(R_f w_0 + \rho\sigma, \sigma),$$

is the utility-maximising level of portfolio risk. Setting $\hat{x}_{\text{eff}} := x_{\text{eff}}(1) = \frac{1}{\rho} V^{-1}\pi$ as the portfolio with unit risk, we conclude that mean-variance efficient portfolios (1.6) satisfy the short-sale constraint (1.3) whenever

$$x_{\text{eff}}^{(n)}(\sigma) = \sigma \hat{x}_{\text{eff}}^{(n)} \geq \chi. \tag{1.7}$$

Since $\chi \leq 0$, the short-sale constraint can only be binding if asset n is shorted in the efficient portfolio with unit risk. We therefore adopt the following assumption.

Assumption 2. *The investor's expected gross returns* $0 \neq \pi \in \mathbb{R}^n$ *are such that* $\langle e_n, V^{-1}\pi \rangle < 0$ *and thus*

$$\langle e_n, \hat{x}_{\text{eff}} \rangle < 0,$$

where $e_n = (0, \dots, 0, 1)^\top \in \mathbb{R}^n$ *denotes the* n*-th canonical basis vector.*

Under Assumption 2, Inequality (1.7) stipulates an upper bound $\underline{\sigma}$ on portfolio risk, above which the short-sale constraint comes into effect. The optimal portfolio (1.6) fulfils the short-sale constraint if and only if its optimal risk σ^* satisfies

$$\sigma^* \leq \frac{\chi}{\langle e_n, \hat{x}_{\text{eff}} \rangle} =: \underline{\sigma}. \tag{1.8}$$

If $\chi < 0$ and thus short-selling of a reasonable size is allowed, the upper bound on the portfolio risk $\underline{\sigma}$ is the ratio between allowed and demanded shares of asset n. On the other hand, if $\chi = 0$ and thus short-selling of asset

[2] The price of risk $\rho := \sqrt{\langle \pi, V^{-1}\pi \rangle}$ can be seen as a subjective measure of return, that the investor demands to bear one unit of risk. The notation will become more clear in Section 1.2 when the efficient frontier is introduced.

[3] The theorem dates back to TOBIN (1958) and LINTNER (1965).

n is prohibited, Assumption 2 together with (1.8) implies that the short-sale constraint is binding whenever the investor participates into the market of risky assets. In this case, the mean-variance efficient portfolios do not satisfy the short-sale constraint and the classical Two-fund Separation theorem becomes invalid. In the next section we therefore determine the solution to the decision problem (1.4) and derive a separation theorem that accounts for constrained short-selling.

1.2 Separation theorem

In this section we study the consequences of short-sale constraints on the *optimal portfolio selection* of an investor with $\mu-\sigma$ preferences. For this purpose, we generalise the classical Two-fund Separation and show that an investor will invest her funds into the risk-free bond and a *constrained-efficient* portfolio. This portfolio is obtained by considering a *value-maximising investor* who maximises expected future wealth, given a prescribed level of risk $\sigma \geq 0$. Formally, her portfolio decision problem is[4]

$$\max_{x \in X} \mathrm{M}(x) \quad \text{s.t.} \quad \mathrm{Sd}(x) \leq \sigma. \tag{1.10}$$

In the following we will show that the optimisation problem (1.10) admits a unique solution if the investor has *non-primitive expectations*.

Definition 1. *The investor's expectations are called* non-primitive *if, on average, she expects a non-zero excess return on at least one unregulated asset, that is*

$$\exists k \in \{1, \ldots, n-1\} \quad \text{s.t.} \quad \bar{q}^{(k)} \neq R_f p^{(k)}.$$

An investor with non-primitive expectations is one who also participates in the security market with risky assets $1, \ldots, n-1$, referred to as the *smaller financial market*. In other words, regulating asset n will not expel the investor from the asset market. Zero excess returns on all unregulated assets on the other hand, represent a rather exceptional case. Nevertheless, for the sake of completeness, the portfolio selection of investors with *primitive expectations* who interact in the financial market to solely trade the regulated asset, is analysed in Appendix A.3.

[4] Similarly, one can consider a *risk-minimising investor* who minimises the standard deviation of future wealth, given a prescribed level of return and the short-sale constraint,

$$\min_{x \in X} \mathrm{Sd}(x) \quad \text{s.t.} \quad \mathrm{M}(x) \geq \mu, \tag{1.9}$$

where $\mu \geq R_f$.

Technically, the assumption of non-primitive expectations implies that the objective function $\mathrm{M}(x)$ and the short-sale constraint function $\langle e_n, x\rangle$ have different gradients as depicted in Figure 1.1. Figure 1.1(a) illustrates that a binding short-sale constraint reduces the set of feasible portfolios, which, in the absence of the constraint is given by the interior of the ellipsoid. If additionally the sales are restricted to be larger than χ, the feasible set shrinks to the blue region inside the ellipsoid. Therefore, the value-maximising investor is forced to hold a constrained-efficient rather than an efficient portfolio. She will thus suffer a loss in return. On the other hand, a risk-minimising investor will assume a higher level of portfolio risk in order to attain the same expected value, see Figure 1.1(b). The set of feasible portfolios reduces to the blue polyhedron whenever the short-sale constraint comes into effect. Consequently, the investor can obtain the constrained-efficient portfolio only at the expense of a larger standard deviation.

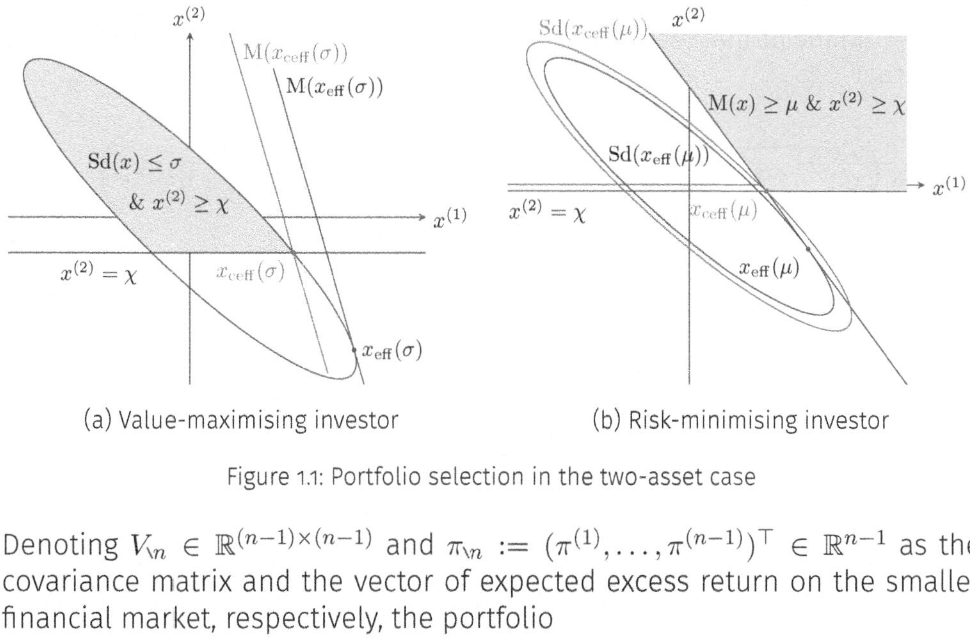

(a) Value-maximising investor (b) Risk-minimising investor

Figure 1.1: Portfolio selection in the two-asset case

Denoting $V_{\setminus n} \in \mathbb{R}^{(n-1)\times(n-1)}$ and $\pi_{\setminus n} := (\pi^{(1)}, \ldots, \pi^{(n-1)})^\top \in \mathbb{R}^{n-1}$ as the covariance matrix and the vector of expected excess return on the smaller financial market, respectively, the portfolio

$$z_{\mathrm{eff}}(\sigma) := \frac{\sigma}{\sqrt{\langle \pi_{\setminus n}, (V_{\setminus n})^{-1} \pi_{\setminus n}\rangle}} (V_{\setminus n})^{-1} \pi_{\setminus n} \in \mathbb{R}^{n-1} \tag{1.11}$$

becomes the (unconstrained) mean-variance efficient portfolio on the financial market with $n-1$ risky assets. Using Equation (1.11), the following theorem characterises constrained-efficient portfolios and shows that the optimisation problem (1.10) admits a unique solution if the investor has non-primitive expectations.

Theorem 1. *Let the hypothesis of Assumption 2 be satisfied and let $\pi^{(k)} \neq 0$ for at least one $k \in \{1, \dots, n-1\}$. Then the optimisation problem (1.10) admits a unique solution which takes the form*[5]

$$x_{\text{ceff}}(\sigma, \chi) = \begin{cases} x_{\text{eff}}(\sigma) & \textit{if } \sigma \leq \underline{\sigma}, \\ \left(z_{\text{eff}}\left(\sqrt{\sigma^2 - \sigma_\chi^2}\right), 0\right)^\top + x_\chi & \textit{if } \sigma > \underline{\sigma}, \end{cases} \tag{1.12}$$

where[6]

$$x_\chi := \frac{\chi}{\langle e_n, V^{-1} e_n \rangle} V^{-1} e_n \quad \textit{and} \quad \sigma_\chi^2 := \mathbb{V}\text{ar}(x_\chi) = \frac{\chi^2}{\langle e_n, V^{-1} e_n \rangle} > \underline{\sigma}^2. \tag{1.13}$$

Moreover, if $\pi = 0$ then $x_{\text{ceff}} = 0$.

Theorem 1 states that the constrained-efficient portfolio $x_{\text{ceff}}(\sigma, \chi)$ consists of a portfolio $(z_{\text{eff}}(\sqrt{\sigma^2 - \sigma_\chi^2}), 0)^\top$ which is mean-variance efficient on the smaller financial market corrected by the portfolio x_χ. In Appendix A.1 we show that

$$\begin{aligned} \left(z_{\text{eff}}\left(\sqrt{\sigma^2 - \sigma_\chi^2}\right), 0\right)^\top &= \frac{\sqrt{\sigma^2 - \sigma_\chi^2}}{\underline{\rho}} \left(V^{-1}\pi - \frac{\langle e_n, V^{-1}\pi \rangle}{\langle e_n, V^{-1} e_n \rangle} V^{-1} e_n\right) \\ &= \frac{\sqrt{\sigma^2 - \sigma_\chi^2}}{\underline{\rho}} W\pi, \end{aligned} \tag{1.14}$$

where

$$W := \left(\begin{array}{c|c} (V_{\setminus n})^{-1} & \begin{matrix} 0 \\ \vdots \\ 0 \end{matrix} \\ \hline 0 \cdots 0 & 0 \end{array} \right),$$

and $\underline{\rho} := \langle \pi, W\pi \rangle$ denotes the price of risk on the smaller financial market. The correction term x_χ is the solution of the following decision problem

$$\min_{x \in \mathbb{R}^n} \text{Sd}(x) \quad \text{s.t.} \quad x^{(n)} = \chi, \tag{1.15}$$

---

[5] If $\pi^{(k)} \neq 0$ for at least one $k \in \{1, \dots, n-1\}$, the Cauchy-Schwarz inequality reads $\langle e_n, V^{-1}\pi \rangle^2 \leq \langle \pi, V^{-1}\pi \rangle \langle e_n, V^{-1} e_n \rangle$, implying

$$\sigma_\chi^2 > \underline{\sigma}^2.$$

[6] Note that $x_\chi = \left(\chi \frac{\langle e_1, V^{-1} e_n \rangle}{\langle e_n, V^{-1} e_n \rangle}, \dots, \chi \frac{\langle e_{n-1}, V^{-1} e_n \rangle}{\langle e_n, V^{-1} e_n \rangle}, \chi\right)$ and thus $x_\chi^{(n)} = \chi$.

and may therefore be viewed as a minimum-variance portfolio with shares of asset n constrained to χ. A proof of this claim is found in Appendix A.2. The portfolio x_χ is proportional to the n-th column of V^{-1} and is identical for all investors who hold the same beliefs regarding the second moments of the return distribution.

If a full ban on short-sales is set, Equations (1.13) imply that $x_\chi = 0$ and $\sigma_\chi = 0$ so that the constrained-efficient portfolio is the mean-variance efficient portfolio on the smaller financial market.

Proposition 1. *Let the hypothesis of Assumption 2 be satisfied and* $\chi = 0$. *Then the optimisation problem* (1.10) *admits a unique solution which takes the form*

$$x_{\text{ceff}}(\sigma) = (z_{\text{eff}}(\sigma), 0)^\top. \tag{1.16}$$

A conventional example in financial literature is the case where the investor assumes risky assets to be pairwise uncorrelated. In this situation the covariance matrix is diagonal.

Example 1. *Consider* $V = \operatorname{diag}(\mathbb{V}\text{ar}(\tilde{q}^{(1)}), \ldots, \mathbb{V}\text{ar}(\tilde{q}^{(n)}))$ *and let* $\sigma > \underline{\sigma}$. *Then* $\langle e_k, V^{-1} e_n \rangle = 0$ *for all* $k \neq n$ *and* $x_\chi = (0, \ldots, 0, \chi)^\top$. *It can easily be shown that*

$$\sigma > \underline{\sigma} \iff \frac{\sigma}{\rho} < \frac{\sqrt{\sigma^2 - \sigma_\chi^2}}{\underline{\rho}}.$$

Thus, the asset demand of any security k satisfies

$$\left| x_{\text{eff}}^{(k)}(\sigma) \right| < \left| x_{\text{ceff}}^{(k)}(\sigma) \right| \quad \text{for all } k \neq n. \tag{1.17}$$

Example 1 shows that an investor who assumes risky assets to be pairwise uncorrelated, will increase the relative amount invested to or borrowed from risky assets, whenever short-selling is restricted. Therefore, a binding short-sale constraint might increase the risk in the financial market.

In order to derive a separation theorem in the presence of short-sale constraints, we first construct the *constrained-efficient frontier*, i.e. the geometric location of risk-return profiles of all constrained-efficient portfolios. For fixed w_0 and $\pi \neq 0$, consider therefore the curve

$$\sigma \mapsto \mathrm{M}(x_{\text{ceff}}(\sigma, \chi)).$$

Inserting $x_{\text{ceff}}(\sigma, \chi)$, as given in Theorem 1, this curve takes the form

$$\mathcal{E}(\sigma) = \begin{cases} R_f w_0 + \rho\sigma & \text{if } \sigma \leq \underline{\sigma}, \\ R_f w_0 + \chi \frac{\langle e_n, V^{-1}\pi \rangle}{\langle e_n, V^{-1} e_n \rangle} + \underline{\rho}\sqrt{\sigma^2 - \sigma_\chi^2} & \text{if } \sigma > \underline{\sigma}, \end{cases} \tag{1.18}$$

where $\underline{\rho} = \sqrt{\langle \pi, W\pi \rangle}$ denotes the price of risk on the smaller financial market.

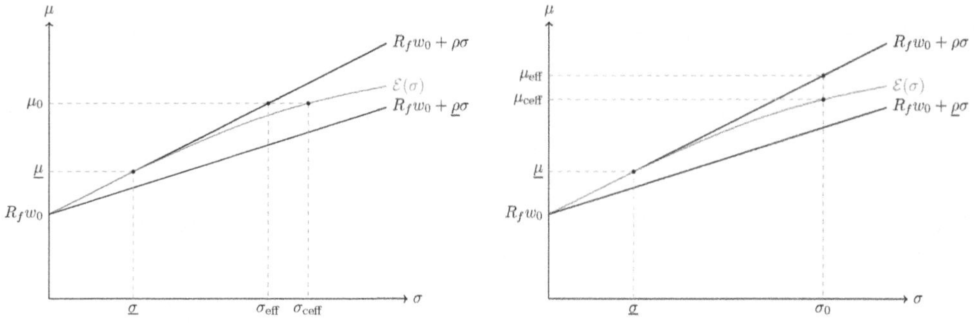

(a) Increase of risk for a given μ_0 (b) Loss in returns for a given σ_0

Figure 1.2: Constrained-efficient frontier

The map $\mathcal{E}$ describes a concave curve in the μ–σ plane which is depicted in Figure 1.2 and its slope may be interpreted as the price of risk in the presence of the short-sale constraint. If short-selling is not binding, $\mathcal{E}$ coincides with the classical *efficient frontier*. On the interval $[0, \underline{\sigma}]$ the frontier is thus a straight line with slope ρ. Whenever the restricted short-sale constraint is binding, $\mathcal{E}$ is bounded and strictly concave on the interval $[\underline{\sigma}, \infty)$. The upper bound is given by the classical efficient frontier $R_f w_0 + \rho\sigma$. The lower bound is given by

$$\mu = R_f w_0 + \underline{\rho}\sigma, \tag{1.19}$$

which is the efficient frontier on the smaller financial market. Note that, if short-selling is prohibited, the slope of $\mathcal{E}$ is given by $\underline{\rho}$ and the constrained-efficient frontier coincides with the linear curve (1.19).

Assuming that short-selling of *more than one* security is forbidden, DYBVIG (1984) proved that the constrained-efficient frontier may have kink points. This result was further extended by MARKOWITZ (1990) who showed that the constrained-efficient frontier is piecewise linear. We contribute to this literature by showing that the linear range corresponds to the efficient frontier on the smaller financial market without the corresponding regulated asset. The properties of $\mathcal{E}$ are summarised in the following lemma.

Lemma 1. *Let the hypothesis of Assumption 2 be satisfied and $\chi < 0$. Then the following holds true:*

1. *The slope of $\mathcal{E}$ is at most ρ and $\mathcal{E}'(\sigma) < \rho$ for all $\sigma > \underline{\sigma}$;*
2. *For all $\sigma > \underline{\sigma}$, $\mathcal{E}$ is strictly concave, i.e. $\mathcal{E}''(\sigma) < 0$ for all $\sigma > \underline{\sigma}$;*

3. *The limiting slope of $\mathcal{E}$ satisfies* $\lim_{\sigma\to\infty} \mathcal{E}'(\sigma) = \underline{\rho} < \rho$.

If $\chi = 0$, *then* $\mathcal{E}(\sigma) = R_f w_0 + \underline{\rho}\sigma$ *for all* $\sigma \in \mathbb{R}_+$.

We are now in a position to formulate a separation theorem for asset demand functions in the presence of constrained short-selling. The classical Two-fund Separation theorem characterises the solution of the investor's unconstrained decision problem (1.5). It states that an investor will choose an efficient portfolio in the sense of Markowitz with a utility-maximising level of risk and invest the rest into the risk-free bond. Taking into account that short-selling of one risky asset is constrained, the Two-fund Separation theorem can be generalised as follows.

Theorem 2 (Separation theorem). *Let the hypotheses of Assumptions 1 and 2 be satisfied and assume in addition that* $\sqrt{\langle \pi, V^{-1}\pi\rangle} < \rho_U(R_f w_0)$. *Then the optimisation problem* (1.4) *admits a unique solution* $x_c^* \in \mathbb{R}^n$.

- *If* $\chi < 0$ *the solution takes the form* $x_c^* = x_{\text{ceff}}(\sigma_c^*, \chi) \in \mathbb{R}^n$, *where*

$$\sigma_c^* = \arg\max_{\sigma\geq 0} U(\mathcal{E}(\sigma), \sigma), \tag{1.20}$$

  is the optimal level of portfolio risk the investor is willing to assume.

- *If* $\chi = 0$, *the solution takes the form* $x_c^* = (z_{\text{eff}}(\sigma_c^*), 0)^\top \in \mathbb{R}^n$, *where*

$$\sigma_c^* = \arg\max_{\sigma\geq 0} U(R_f w_0 + \underline{\rho}\sigma, \sigma) \tag{1.21}$$

  is the optimal level of portfolio risk the investor is willing to assume.

Theorem 2 shows that in the presence of a short-sale constraint, the investor will choose a constrained-efficient portfolio $x_{\text{ceff}}(\sigma_c^*, \chi)$ with a utility-maximising level of portfolio risk $\sigma_c^* > 0$ and invest the rest into the risk-free bond. In particular, two investors having different risk preferences but homogeneous beliefs $(\bar{q}, V)$ regarding the future returns of risky securities will hold collinear portfolios only if short-selling is prohibited. However, if short-selling is restricted, the constrained-efficient portfolio depends non-linearly on the level of portfolio risk. Hence, two intermediaries with the same beliefs but different risk preferences will no longer invest into a mutual fund. The separation theorem is depicted in Figure 1.3. A rigorous proof of the separation theorem is given in Appendix A.1.

The following example focuses on the influence of the short-sale constraint on the asset demand and the risk taking behaviour of an investor. The preferences are considered to be linear in mean and variance.

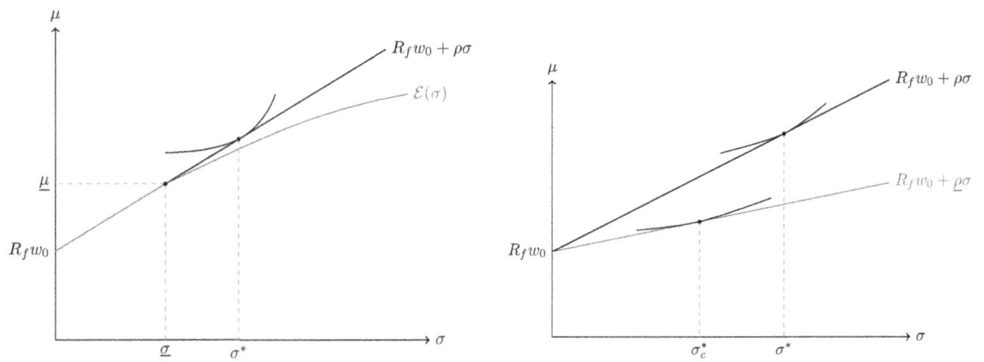

(a) Restricted short-selling (b) Prohibited short-selling

Figure 1.3: Separation theorem

Example 2. *Consider the standard case of linear mean-variance preferences, described by*

$$U(\mu, \sigma) = \mu - \frac{1}{2a}\sigma^2,$$

where the parameter a scales the investor's degree of risk tolerance. The first order condition implies that the optimal portfolio risk of an investor is $\sigma^* = a\sqrt{\langle \pi, V^{-1}\pi \rangle}$ if short-selling is unrestricted. Since the corresponding optimal portfolio is $x^* = aV^{-1}\pi$, the short-sale constraint is binding whenever $\langle e_n, x^* \rangle = a\langle e_n, V^{-1}\pi \rangle \leq \chi$. The first order condition for a binding short-sale constraint takes the form

$$\frac{\sigma}{a} \overset{!}{=} \mathcal{E}'(\sigma) = \sigma\sqrt{\frac{\langle e_n, V^{-1}\pi \rangle^2 - \rho^2 \langle e_n, V^{-1}e_n \rangle}{\chi^2 - \sigma^2 \langle e_n, V^{-1}e_n \rangle}}.$$

Solving for σ, the optimal portfolio risk becomes

$$\sigma_c^* = \begin{cases} a\sqrt{\langle \pi, V^{-1}\pi \rangle} & \text{if } a\langle e_n, V^{-1}\pi \rangle \geq \chi, \\ a\sqrt{\langle \pi, V^{-1}\pi \rangle - \left(\frac{a^2\langle e_n, V^{-1}\pi \rangle^2 - \chi^2}{\langle e_n, V^{-1}e_n \rangle}\right)} & \text{otherwise.} \end{cases} \tag{1.22}$$

Thus, the investor will reduce her portfolio risk in response to a binding short-sale constraint. For the constrained-optimal portfolio the separation theorem implies

$$\begin{aligned} x_c^* &= x_{\text{ceff}}(\sigma_c^*, \chi) \\ &= aV^{-1}\pi - \frac{a\langle e_n, V^{-1}\pi \rangle}{\langle e_n, V^{-1}e_n \rangle} V^{-1}e_n + \frac{\chi}{\langle e_n, V^{-1}e_n \rangle} V^{-1}e_n. \end{aligned} \tag{1.23}$$

Inserting $x^* = aV^{-1}\pi$ into (1.23), we obtain

$$x_c^* - x^* = \underbrace{\frac{\chi - \langle e_n, x^* \rangle}{\langle e_n, V^{-1} e_n \rangle}}_{\geq 0} V^{-1} e_n. \tag{1.24}$$

Therefore, if the short-sale constraint it binding, so that $\chi > \langle e_n, x^* \rangle$, the investor will demand more shares of any risky asset $k \in \{1, \ldots, n\}$ if and only if

$$\langle e_k, V^{-1} e_n \rangle > 0. \tag{1.25}$$

Whether or not the investor will increase the asset demand depends solely on investor's estimates of the second moment of the return distribution. In the case of two risky assets, the condition $\langle e_1, V^{-1} e_2 \rangle > 0$ holds if and only if $\mathbb{Cov}\left(\tilde{q}^{(1)}, \tilde{q}^{(2)}\right) < 0$. This is in accordance with conventional economic intuition that in the presence of a short-sale constraint, an investor will demand more shares of the unregulated stock if and only if the assets move in opposite directions. If the number of securities on a financial market is large, the computation of $\langle e_k, V^{-1} e_n \rangle$ is rather complicated and cumbersome. The case of three risky assets, for example, shows that $\langle e_1, V^{-1} e_3 \rangle > 0$ if and only if

$$\mathbb{Cov}\left(\tilde{q}^{(1)}, \tilde{q}^{(3)}\right) \mathbb{Var}\left(\tilde{q}^{(2)}\right) > \mathbb{Cov}\left(\tilde{q}^{(1)}, \tilde{q}^{(2)}\right) \mathbb{Cov}\left(\tilde{q}^{(2)}, \tilde{q}^{(3)}\right).$$

The minimum-variance portfolio defined in Theorem 1, however, provides a simple and interesting possibility to interpret Inequality (1.25). Recall that the minimum variance portfolio is given by $x_\chi = \frac{\chi}{\langle e_n, V^{-1} e_n \rangle} V^{-1} e_n$. Since $\chi < 0$, we can conclude that $\langle e_k, V^{-1} e_n \rangle > 0$ if and only if $\langle e_k, x_\chi \rangle < 0$. Thus, the investor will demand more shares of asset k if and only if the asset is a short position in the minimum-variance portfolio x_χ.

1.3 Risk-taking behaviour

The separation theorem reduced the multivariate existence problem (1.4) of finding optimal portfolios to a univariate problem of determining the optimal portfolio risk. Consequently, this section is concerned with the impact of the short-sale constraint on the optimal risk-return characteristics of portfolios. A common hypothesis in empirical works states that the investor who is allowed to sell short, will hold a portfolio with lower portfolio risk than the restricted investor (see e.g. GRUBE AND BEEDLES (1981)). Our aim is to verify the validity of this statement by applying basic microeconomic principles, so that risk-taking behaviour of an investor can be analysed in a two-commodity space with the commodities risk, σ, and expected return, μ. In view of the separation theorem, the portfolio risk in the presence of the short-sale constraint an investor is willing to assume may formally be defined by

$$\varphi_c(w_0, \pi, \chi) := \arg\max_{\sigma \geq 0} U(\mathcal{E}(\sigma), \sigma),$$

so that the constrained-optimal risk is $\sigma_c^* = \varphi_c(w_0, \pi, \chi)$.

A key insight of the mean-variance analysis into the risk-taking behaviour is the observation that restricted short-selling has the same effect as providing the investor with a higher endowment and lowering the price of risk. Figure 1.4(a) illustrates this by decomposing a binding short-sale constraint into a price effect, PE, caused by a decrease in the price of risk, and an endowment effect, EE, due to an increase of endowment.[7] If, however, a full ban on short-selling is implemented, the constrained-efficient frontier is represented by a line with a smaller price of risk. Hence, prohibited short-selling has only a price effect. This case is shown in Figure 1.4(b). These observations may be formalised as follows.

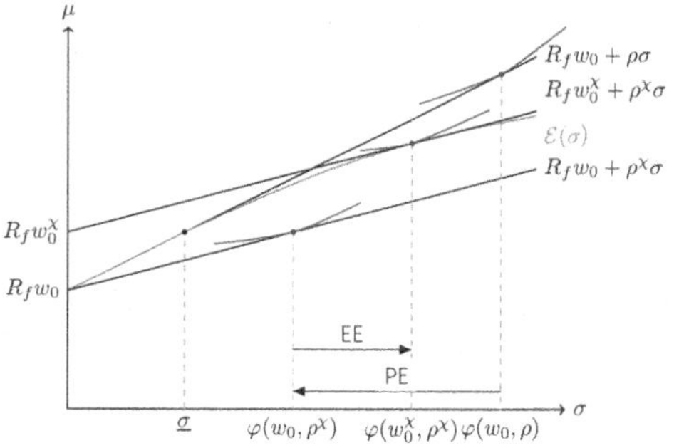

(a) Restricted short-selling

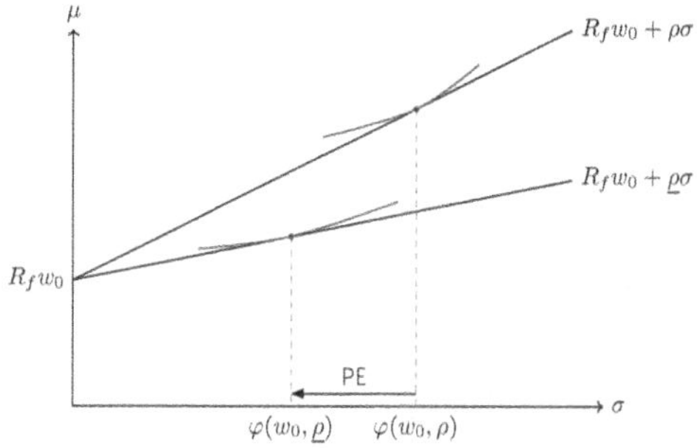

(b) Prohibited short-selling

Figure 1.4: Effect of the short-sale constraint

Lemma 2. *Let the hypotheses of Assumptions 1 and 2 be satisfied. Then the following holds true:*

1. *If $\chi < 0$, there exist a price of risk ρ^χ and an endowment w_0^χ such that*

$$\sigma_c^* = \varphi_c(w_0, \pi, \chi) = \varphi(w_0^\chi, \rho^\chi).$$

Moreover,

$$\rho^\chi = \mathcal{E}'(\sigma_c^*) \leq \rho \quad and \quad w_0^\chi = \mathcal{E}(\sigma_c^*) - \mathcal{E}'(\sigma_c^*)\sigma_c^* \geq w_0,$$

[7] The decomposition is analogous to the well-known Slutsky decomposition in microeconomics. Details are relegated to Appendix A.4.

and both inequalities are strict whenever the short-sale constraint is binding.

2. *If $\chi = 0$, the optimal level of portfolio risk an investor is willing to assume is given by*
$$\sigma_c^* = \varphi_c(w_0, \pi, 0) = \varphi(w_0, \underline{\rho}).$$

Proof. Let $\chi < 0$, then the first-order condition is $S(\mathcal{E}(\sigma_c^*), \sigma_c^*) = \mathcal{E}'(\sigma_c^*)$. Set $\rho^\chi = \mathcal{E}'(\sigma_c^*)$ and choose w_0^χ such that $\mathcal{E}(\sigma_c^*) = w_0^\chi + \rho^\chi \sigma_c^*$. Since by, Lemma 1, $\rho^\chi < \rho$, the claim follows directly from the separation theorem. If $\chi = 0$, the constrained-efficient frontier is given by $\mathcal{E}(\sigma) = R_f w_0 + \underline{\rho}\sigma$, which immediately yields the second claim. □

The risk-taking behaviour of an investor with $\mu-\sigma$ preferences in the absence of short-sale restrictions has been studied in WENZELBURGER (2010), see also, DANA (1999) and HENS ET AL. (2002). The main results are summarised in the following.

Proposition 2. *Let the hypotheses of Assumption 1 be satisfied. Then, for all $w_0 \geq 0$ and $S(R_f w_0, 0) \leq \rho < \rho_U(R_f w_0)$, the following holds true:*

(i) $\frac{\partial \varphi(w_0, \rho)}{\partial \rho} > 0$ *if and only if*
$$\frac{\partial S}{\partial \mu}(R_f w_0 + \rho\varphi(w_0, \rho), \varphi(w_0, \rho))\varphi(w_0, \rho) < 1.$$

(ii) $\frac{\partial \varphi(w_0, \rho)}{\partial w_0} > 0$ *if and only if*
$$\frac{\partial S}{\partial \mu}(R_f w_0 + \rho\varphi(w_0, \rho), \varphi(w_0, \rho)) < 0.$$

Lemma 2 and Proposition 2 can be used to analyse the impact of restricted and prohibited short-selling on the investor's risk-taking behaviour. Proposition 2 ensures that the willingness to assume risk φ must be increasing in the price of risk ρ, if φ is increasing in wealth w_0. As a consequence, the risk-taking behaviour of an investor can be classified into three categories. In the first one, φ is decreasing in w_0 and increasing in ρ; in the second, φ is decreasing in both w_0 and ρ. The third one finally, describes the case where φ is increasing in both w_0 and ρ.[8] In the following subsection we will discuss how the investor's willingness to assume risk is affected by implementing restrictions on short-sales.

[8] The analogy to standard microeconomics is that an inferior good may or may not be a Giffen good, while a normal good is never a Giffen good.

1.3.1 Restricted short-selling

As previously shown, a restricted short-sale constraint has the same effect as providing the investor with higher endowment and lowering the price of risk. Moreover, Proposition 2 showed that price and endowment effects may not be aligned. Thus, whether restricted short-selling will reduce the portfolio risk depends on the magnitudes of these effects. In category-1, price and endowment effects are aligned, so that $\varphi(w_0^X, \rho^X) < \varphi(w_0, \rho)$ as illustrated in Figure 1.5(a). In the other two categories, price and endowment effects are not aligned, so that either $\varphi(w_0, \rho) < \varphi(w_0, \rho^X)$ and $\varphi(w_0, \rho^X) > \varphi(w_0^X, \rho^X)$ (category-2) or $\varphi(w_0, \rho) > \varphi(w_0, \rho^X)$ and $\varphi(w_0, \rho^X) < \varphi(w_0^X, \rho^X)$ (category-3) are possible. The following example illustrates category-1 and category-2 investors.

Example 3. *Consider the family of additive separable utility functions of the form*[9]

$$U(\mu, \sigma) = u(\mu) - \gamma v(\sigma), \qquad \gamma \geq 0, \tag{1.26}$$

where u is strictly increasing and concave, v is strictly increasing and convex, and either u is strictly concave or v is strictly convex. The parameter γ scales the degree of risk aversion. The marginal rate of substitution is $S_\gamma(\mu, \sigma) = \gamma \frac{v'(\sigma)}{u'(\mu)}$, yielding

$$\frac{\partial S_\gamma}{\partial \mu}(\mu, \sigma) = -\frac{\gamma v'(\sigma) u''(\mu)}{u'(\mu)^2} \geq 0.$$

By Proposition 2 (ii), the willingness to assume risk φ is decreasing in w_0. Moreover, Condition (i) of Proposition 2 takes the form

$$\frac{u''(R_f w_0 + \mu)\mu}{u'(R_f w_0 + \mu)} > -1.$$

It follows that in the quasi-linear case, in which $u(\mu) = \mu$, the function φ is decreasing in w_0 and increasing in ρ. This characterises the category-1 investor. An immediate consequence is that all investors whose risk preferences are described by a quasi-linear utility function will reduce portfolio risk whenever the restricted short-sale constraint is binding (see Figure 1.5(a)). For $u(\mu) = \frac{\mu}{1+\mu}$ and $v(\sigma) = \sigma$, the willingness to assume risk φ is decreasing in both w_0 and ρ and represents the behaviour of a category-2 investor. Figure 1.5(b) illustrates the latter case in which a negative price effect dominates a positive endowment effect, thus leading to an increase in portfolio risk.

[9] Any monotonic transformation of a separable utility function, where $\tilde{U}(\mu, \sigma) = h(u(\mu) - v(\sigma))$ with $h' > 0$, will lead to the same risk aversion $S(\mu, \sigma) = \frac{v'(\sigma)}{u'(\mu)}$ and hence to the same result.

Example 3 shows that a restricted short-sale constraint will prompt investors with quasi-linear preferences to reduce portfolio risk. This result contradicts the aforementioned empirical findings presented in GRUBE AND BEEDLES (1981). This contradiction may be attributed to the fact that additive separable utility functions are unsatisfactory, since conventional wisdom would expect richer investors to engage in riskier investments. The next example is taken from

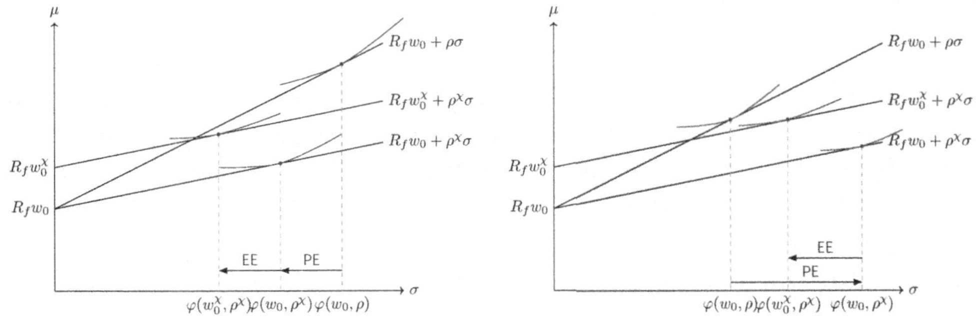

(a) Category-1 investor (b) Category-2 investor

Figure 1.5: Endowment effect (EE) and price effect (PE)

HUNANYAN AND WENZELBURGER (2018A) and provides a class of utility functions that features investors who increase portfolio risk when better endowed.

Example 4. *Consider utility functions of the form*

$$U_\gamma(\mu, \sigma) = \frac{\mu - \mu_0}{v(\gamma\sigma)}$$

which for fixed $\gamma > 0$ are defined on the set

$$\mathbb{D}_\gamma := \left\{(\mu, \sigma) \in \mathbb{R}_+^2 : \mu \leq \mu_0 \text{ and } v(\gamma\sigma) \geq 0\right\}.$$

The function $v(\sigma)$ is assumed to be strictly positive, strictly decreasing, strictly concave and twice differentiable with $\lim_{\sigma \to \sigma_0} v'(\sigma) = -\infty$.[10] *The marginal rate of substitution is*

$$S_\gamma(\mu, \sigma) = (\mu - \mu_0)\frac{\gamma v'(\gamma\sigma)}{v(\gamma\sigma)} > 0,$$

so that $\frac{\partial S_\gamma}{\partial \mu} = \gamma\frac{v'(\gamma\sigma)}{v(\gamma\sigma)} < 0$. Proposition 2 implies that the willingness to assume risk, denoted by φ_γ, is increasing in both w_0 and ρ. Figure 1.6(a) depicts the case of such a category-3 investor, where a positive price effect dominates a negative endowment effect.

[10] Since $U_\gamma(\mu, \sigma) < 0$ for $\mu < \mu_0$, the function v cannot be transformed to an additive separable utility function.

Examples 3 and 4 illustrate that the effectiveness of a restricted short-sale constraint in reducing portfolio risk depends on the interplay between the price and endowment effect. If, however, short-selling is prohibited, the constrained-efficient frontier becomes a line and the analysis of the risk taking behaviour can be simplified.

1.3.2 Prohibited short-selling

As shown in Lemma 2, a full ban on short-sales entails merely a price effect. A decrease in the optimal risk can then be obtained if and only if the willingness to assume risk increases in ρ. Consequently, a category-1 investor will reduce portfolio risk in the presence of the short-sale constraint. The same effect can now be observed for a category-3 investor. However, as the following example shows, the ban has an adverse effect on a category-2 investor, who may attempt to outweigh the losses in profits by increasing portfolio risk.

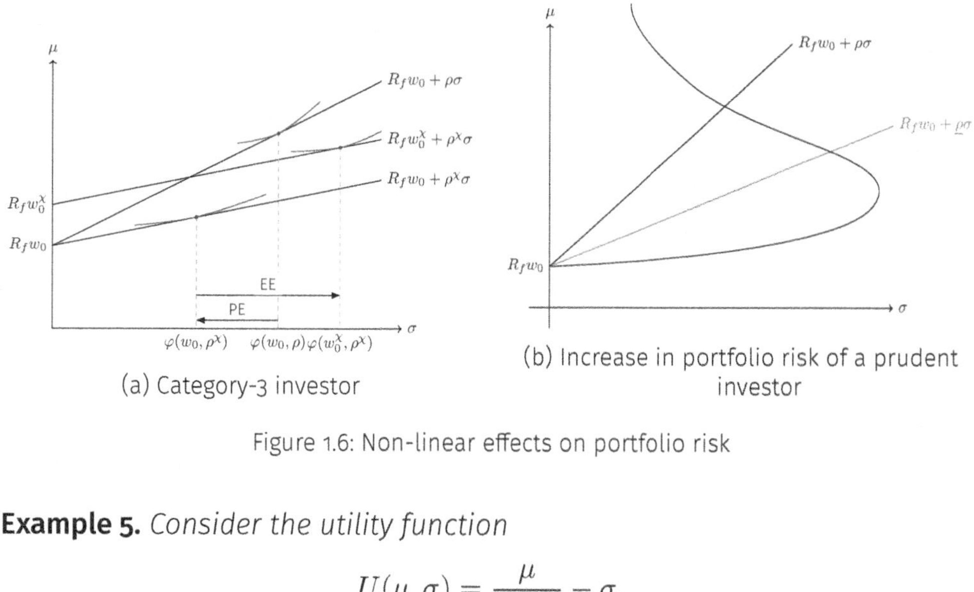

(a) Category-3 investor

(b) Increase in portfolio risk of a prudent investor

Figure 1.6: Non-linear effects on portfolio risk

Example 5. *Consider the utility function*

$$U(\mu, \sigma) = \frac{\mu}{1+\mu} - \sigma,$$

defined for $\mu > -1$ and $\sigma \geq 0$ and assume that short-selling is forbidden. The willingness to assume risk is

$$\varphi(w_0, \rho) = \max\left\{\frac{\sqrt{\rho} - (R_f w_0 + 1)}{\rho}, 0\right\}. \tag{1.27}$$

The function φ characterises the risk-taking behaviour of an investor who will trade risky assets whenever the price of risk is high enough, i.e. $\rho >$

$(R_f w_0+1)^2$. The willingness to assume risk (1.27) is increasing for $\rho \in [(R_f w_0+1)^2, \rho_{\max}(w_0)]$ and decreasing for $\rho \geq \rho_{\max}(w_0)$, where $\rho_{\max}(w_0) := 4(R_f w_0 + 1)^2$. Hence, if $\underline{\rho} > \rho_{\max}(w_0)$, a binding short-sale constraints will force prudent investors to take a higher level of portfolio risk. These findings are illustrated in Figure 1.6(b).

	Restricted short-selling	Prohibited short-selling
Category-1	$\sigma_c^* < \sigma^*$	$\sigma_c^* < \sigma^*$
Category-2	$\sigma_c^* < \sigma^* \Leftrightarrow PE < EE$	$\sigma_c^* > \sigma^*$
Category-3	$\sigma_c^* < \sigma^* \Leftrightarrow PE > EE$	$\sigma_c^* < \sigma^*$

Table 1.1: Restricted vs. prohibited short-selling

Table 1.1 summarises the results of this section. It shows that the empirical hypothesis of taking larger portfolio risk in the presence of a short-sale constraint depends on the type of regulation (i.e. restriction or prohibition of short-sales) as well as the investor's preferences. The prohibited short-sale constraint will reduce the portfolio risk if and only if the willingness to assume risk increases in ρ. If, however, short-selling is restricted, a reduction of the portfolio risk depends on the interplay of price and endowment effects.

1.4 Default risk

Financial literature (see among others ROCHET (1992)) emphasises that the coefficient of variation, which measures the portfolio's expected return per unit of standard deviation, is a suitable measure of an investor's default probability. Consequently, a larger portfolio risk, with a constant or declining expected return, leads to a larger probability of default. The aim of this section is thus to shed new light on the interplay between the risk-taking behaviour and default risk of portfolio managing investors.

Recall that the future endowment of an investor who chooses a portfolio $x \in \mathbb{R}^n$ at prices $p \in \mathbb{R}^n$ is given by

$$\tilde{w}_1(x^*) = R_f w_0 + \langle \tilde{q} - R_f p, x \rangle.$$

The default risk of the investor is formally given by the probability that future wealth $\tilde{w}_1(x)$ is negative. In terms of the centralised random variable $\frac{\tilde{w}_1(x) - \mathrm{M}(x)}{\mathrm{Sd}(x)}$ with mean 0 and standard deviation 1, the default probability of an investor is defined next.

Definition 2. *The default probability of an investor holding the portfolio x of risky assets is given by*

$$\Pi(x) := \text{Prob}(\tilde{w}_1(x) < 0) = \text{Prob}\left(\frac{\tilde{w}_1(x) - \mathrm{M}(x)}{\mathrm{Sd}(x)} < -\frac{\mathrm{M}(x)}{\mathrm{Sd}(x)}\right).$$

In order to compare default probabilities associated with different portfolios of assets and liabilities, we restrict our further analysis to the case of elliptically distributed returns $\tilde{q}$.

Assumption 3. *The gross returns $\tilde{q}$ are multivariate elliptically distributed, $\tilde{q} \sim \mathcal{E}_n(\overline{q}, V)$, where $\overline{q} \in \mathbb{R}^n_+$ is the vector of mean gross returns and V the covariance matrix of gross returns.*

It is well known (e.g. see HÄRDLE AND SIMAR (2012)) that if $\tilde{q}$ is elliptically distributed then so does the final wealth $\tilde{w}_1(x)$ for every portfolio x.[11]

Let $\Phi_{0,1}$ denote the cumulative distribution function of a univariate elliptically distributed random variable with zero mean and variance 1. Then the default probability of an investor holding the portfolio $x \in \mathbb{R}^n$ is $\Phi_{0,1}\left(-\frac{\mathrm{M}(x)}{\mathrm{Sd}(x)}\right)$. The monotonicity of the cumulative distribution function $\Phi_{0,1}$ now yields a necessary and sufficient condition for a reduction in default risk of an investor.

Lemma 3. *Let the hypotheses of Assumptions 1 and 3 be satisfied and $\rho < \rho_U(R_f w_0)$. Then a binding short-sale constraint reduces the investor's default risk if and only if*

$$\frac{\sigma_c^*}{\mathcal{E}\left(\sigma_c^*\right)} < \frac{\sigma^*}{R_f w_0 + \rho\sigma^*}, \tag{1.28}$$

where σ_c^* is the constrained-optimal portfolio risk and σ^* denotes the optimal portfolio risk of the investor when short-selling is permitted.

Lemma 3 is illustrated in Figure 1.7 and shows the one-to-one relationship between default risk and optimal portfolio risk. The coefficient of variation is represented by the secant connecting the origin with the risk-return profile. The optimal levels of risk σ^* and σ_c^* determine the risk-return profiles $(R_f w_0 + \rho\sigma^*, \sigma^*)$, $(\mathcal{E}(\sigma_c^*), \sigma_c^*)$, respectively and thus also the effectiveness of short-sale constraints in reducing the investor's default risk.

In Section 1.1 we demonstrated that these constraints diminish the set of feasible portfolios, thereby reducing the profitability of the investment opportunities in terms of expected returns. A higher level of portfolio risk will

[11] The most common example of an elliptical distribution is the multivariate normal distribution. This class of distributions has several interesting properties. Most important in our context is the fact that any linear combination of elliptically distributed variables is again elliptically distributed. Further details are explained in Appendix A.5.

enlarge the coefficient of variation of future wealth, thus increase the default risk. This observation is formalised in the following.

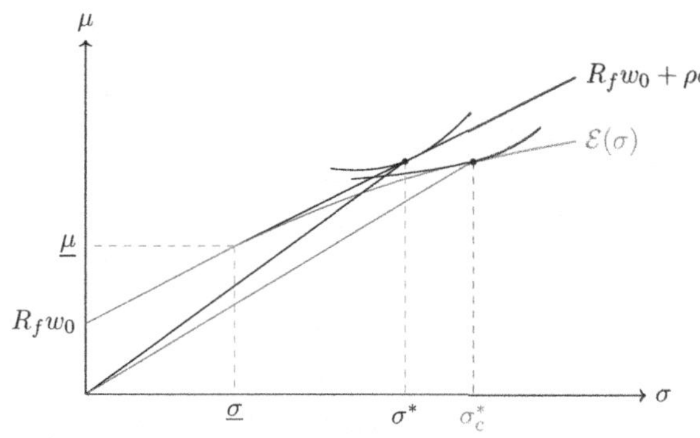

Figure 1.7: Increase in portfolio risk and default risk

Corollary 1. *Let the hypothesis of Assumption 3 be satisfied. If an investor assumes more portfolio risk in the presence of the short-sale constraint, $\sigma_c^* > \sigma^*$, she is more likely to default.*

Proof. If $\sigma_c^* > \sigma^*$, the coefficient of variation increases according to

$$\frac{\sigma^*}{R_f w_0 + \rho\sigma^*} < \frac{\sigma_c^*}{R_f w_0 + \rho\sigma_c^*} < \frac{\sigma_c^*}{\mathcal{E}(\sigma_c^*)}.$$

□

Corollary 1 implies that the investor must scale down portfolio risk in order to reduce default risk. Therefore it only provides a necessary condition for the reduction of default risk. To attain a sufficient condition, we define σ_u as the portfolio risk which satisfies the short-sale constraint and leads to the same default risk as σ^*. Formally, σ_u is given by the solution of the following equation

$$\frac{\sigma_u}{\mathcal{E}(\sigma_u)} = \frac{\sigma^*}{R_f w_0 + \rho\sigma^*}.$$

As illustrated in Figure 1.8(b), the risk profile $(\mathcal{E}(\sigma_u), \sigma_u)$ is the intersection point of the constrained-efficient frontier $\mathcal{E}(\sigma)$ and the secant connecting the origin with $(\sigma^*, R_f w_0 + \rho\sigma^*)$. The next theorem shows that a binding short-sale constraint will reduce the investor's default risk if and only if $\sigma_c^* < \sigma_u$.

Theorem 3. *Let the hypotheses of Assumptions 1, 2 and 3 be satisfied. Then the short-sale constraint will reduce the investor's default risk if and only if*

$$S(\mathcal{E}(\sigma_u), \sigma_u) > \mathcal{E}'(\sigma_u). \tag{1.29}$$

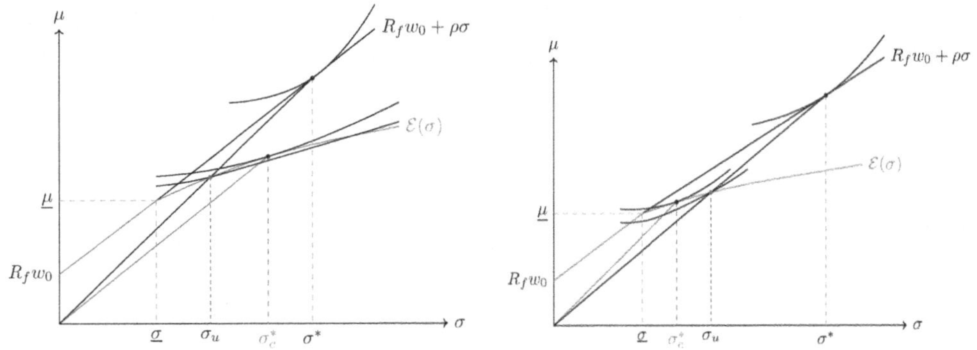

(a) Increase in default probability (b) Decrease in default probability

Figure 1.8: Decrease in portfolio risk

Proof. As argued above, the default risk of the investor subject to the short-sale constraint is lower than her default risk in the absence of the constraint if and only if her constrained-optimal portfolio risk σ_c^* is less than σ_u. Using the first order condition for optimal portfolio risk, this is the case if and only if (1.29) holds. □

Theorem 3 states that an investor is less likely to default, if her risk aversion, given by the marginal rate of substitution between risk and return $S(\mathcal{E}(\sigma_u), \sigma_u)$, is higher than the price of risk $\mathcal{E}'(\sigma_u)$. In this case, an investor will accept the loss in returns that is needed to reduce default risk. Due to the non-linearity of $\mathcal{E}$ the portfolio risk σ_u cannot be computed in general. However, in case of prohibited short-selling, the constrained-efficient frontier is linear with slope $\underline{\rho}$ and σ_u is given by

$$\sigma_u = \frac{R_f w_0}{R_f w_0 + (\rho - \underline{\rho})\sigma^*}.$$

For the remainder of this section we provide a comparative-static analysis to investigate the statement, that a stronger regulation in terms of a smaller short-selling threshold will reduce default risk. Intuitively, a reduction of default risk can only be achieved by a sufficiently elastic reduction of portfolio risk that lowers the coefficient of variation of future wealth. The coefficient of variation of future wealth in the presence of the short-sale constraint is $\mathrm{CV}_c(\chi) := \frac{\varphi_c(w_0,\pi,\chi)}{\mathcal{E}(\varphi_c(w_0,\pi,\chi),\chi)}$. Denoting the elasticity of the willingness to assume risk φ_c w.r.t. the short-selling threshold χ by

$$\varepsilon_{\varphi_c}(\chi) := \frac{\frac{\partial \varphi_c}{\partial \chi}(w_0, \pi, \chi)\chi}{\varphi_c(w_0, \pi, \chi)},$$

the following theorem shows that the required reduction is obtained only if $\varepsilon_{\varphi_c}(\chi) \geq 1$.

Theorem 4. *Let the hypotheses of Assumptions 1, 2, and 3 be satisfied. Then the default probability of an investor decreases with χ, if $\varepsilon_{\varphi_c}(\chi) \geq 1$.*

The proof is given in Appendix A.1. Example 6 applies Theorem 4 to the case of linear mean-variance preferences.

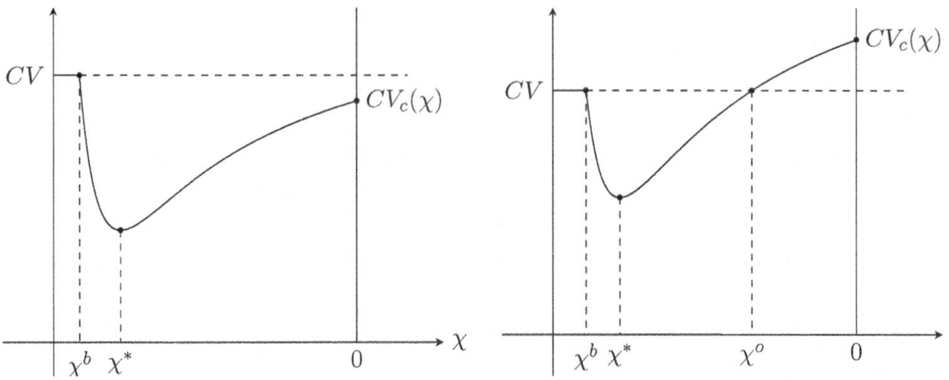

(a) Low risk-tolerance, $a \leq \bar{a}$ (b) High risk-tolerance, $a > \bar{a}$

Figure 1.9: The effect of χ on the default risk

Example 6. *Consider the linear mean-variance preferences $U(\mu, \sigma) = \mu - \frac{1}{2a}\sigma^2$, where a denotes the risk tolerance. In the presence of the short-sale constraint the willingness to assume risk is*

$$\varphi_c(w_0, \pi, \chi) = \begin{cases} a\rho & \text{if } a\langle e_n, V^{-1}\pi\rangle \geq \chi, \\ \sqrt{a^2\underline{\rho}^2 + \frac{\chi^2}{\langle e_n, V^{-1}e_n\rangle}} & \text{otherwise,} \end{cases}$$

where $\underline{\rho} = \langle \pi, W\pi\rangle$. For a given endowment w_0, the short-sale constraint is binding whenever χ is set above $\chi^b := a\langle e_n, V^{-1}\pi\rangle$. The coefficient of variation $\mathrm{CV}_c(\chi)$ of future wealth is then a quadratic function of χ that attains its unique minimum at

$$\chi^* := \chi^b \frac{a\underline{\rho}^2}{a\underline{\rho}^2 + R_f w_0} > \chi^b.$$

Since $\mathrm{CV}_c'(\chi^b) < 0$, regulation reduces default risk whenever $\chi \in [\chi^b, \chi^*]$. Figure 1.9(a) depicts a situation in which the investor is sufficiently risk averse, and less likely to default when short-selling is restricted, regardless of how χ is set. This case occurs for all

$$a \leq \bar{a} := \frac{R_f w_0}{\rho\underline{\rho}}.$$

In Figure 1.9(b) the investor is more likely to default for any short-selling threshold χ above χ^o. This case occurs only if $a > \bar{a}$.

This section's outcome suggest that the enforcement of a short-sale constraint may increase the default risk of investors. However, this unintended effect does not occur in a systematic way[12] but rather depends on market conditions and investor's risk-preferences. From a regulatory point of view, our results are of limited value, since the investor's preferences are, not directly observable. However, following HUNANYAN AND WENZELBURGER (2018A), the results of this section can be generalised to the case of an investor with non-efficient and thus non-optimal risk profiles (μ, σ).

So far we studied the consequences of short-sale constraints on an investor's *individual* decision problem. We showed that the multivariate decision problem to find utility maximising portfolios can be reduced to finding an optimal level of risk. This risk-taking behaviour in turn, affects the investor's *individual* default risk. However, on a financial market where a variety of heterogeneous investors interact, short-sale constraints affect the equilibrium asset prices. Therefore, in the following chapter, we formulate the market structure and examine the consequences of short-sale constraints on the equilibrium prices.

[12] In order to reduce default risk of a portfolio managing investor in a systematic way, HUNANYAN AND WENZELBURGER (2018B) proposed a new regulatory policy that forces the investor to reduce default risk by directly restricting the coefficient of variation. Due to its invariance of changes in market conditions, the regulation of the coefficient of variation appears to be a robust regulatory policy.

2 CAPM Equilibrium

The United States Securities and Exchange Commission (SEC) adopted the short-sale rule to achieve the objective of "preventing short-selling at successively lower prices, thus eliminating short-selling as a tool for driving the market down".[1] In other words, the justification for short-selling restrictions is the prevention of a precipitous downward spiral in prices.

The traditional form of the CAPM presumed investors with homogeneous beliefs regarding the pair $(\bar{q}, V)$.[2] However, this assumption is strong and does not explain short positions. SHARPE (1964), LINTNER (1969) and ROSS (1977) showed that in equilibrium all investors hold shares of the market portfolio, which by definition, has non-negative entries. Consequently, homogeneous expectations cannot explain short positions and asset prices remain unaffected by the short-sale constraint. The desired effect of overpricing[3] has however been confirmed by several empirical studies (see among others CHOIE AND HWANG (1994), BOEHME ET AL. (2006), NAGEL (2005)). From a theoretical perspective, the overpricing hypothesis was mentioned first by MILLER (1977) who considered a simplified financial market with one risky asset and investors with heterogeneous expectations regarding the first two moments of the distribution of the gross return. The author argued that the constraint prevents pessimists to short-sale the asset. Optimistic opinions will then be overrepresented in the market leading to overpriced securities. The overpricing hypothesis is recognised also in recent financial literature with great acceptance (see for example the dynamic models ANUFRIEV AND TUINSTRA (2013) and DERCOLE AND RADI (2014)). However, in all these works the financial market is assumed to contain *solely one* risky asset.

[1] See Exchange Act Release No. 13091 (Dec. 21, 1976), 41 Fed. Reg. 56530 (Dec. 28, 1976)

[2] The financial literature addressed the existence and uniqueness of asset-market equilibria in the traditional CAPM with homogeneous beliefs and its extensions with great generality, e.g., see NIELSEN (1988, 1990A,1990B), ALLINGHAM (1991), DANA (1993, 1999), and HENS ET AL. (2002), WENZELBURGER (2010) or KOCH-MEDINA AND WENZELBURGER (2018).

[3] We make use of the terms "overpricing" or "overvaluation" whenever short-selling restrictions increase the price of risky assets above those which would occur in a world with no restrictions. Equivalently, the terms "underpricing" or "undervaluation" will be used when short-selling restrictions decrease the price of risky assets.

G. Hunanyan, *The Consequences of Short-Sale Constraints on the Stability of Financial Markets*, Finanzwirtschaft, Banken und Bankmanagement | Finance, Banks and Bank Management, https://doi.org/10.1007/978-3-658-27956-1_3

The most notable and general work about equilibrium asset prices on a financial market with short-sale constraints has been carried out by JARROW (1980). By means of a counterexample, Jarrow contradicted Miller's overpricing hypothesis showing that a decline in aggregate demand can result from a *substitution effect*, i.e. binding short-sale constraints may affect the demand of substitute securities.

The present chapter aims to generalise Jarrow's example to a theoretical framework which allows us to analyse the consequences of short-sale constraints on equilibrium asset prices. This chapter is structured as follows: Section 2.1 establishes existence and uniqueness of equilibrium asset prices for an arbitrary but finite number of investors, which are constrained by short-selling limitations. For the case of two investors, Section 2.2 derives an explicit characterisation of the equilibrium prices. We show that overpricing or underpricing solely depends on the investors second moment beliefs. Section 2.3 considers the case of three and more investors showing that in that case the form of equilibrium asset prices cannot be determined without use of an algorithmic procedure.

We consider a financial market in which I investors with heterogeneous preferences and endowments interact. The investor i's initial endowment is denoted by $w_0^i \in \mathbb{R}$ and her preferences are described by the linear mean-variance utility function $U^i(\mu, \sigma) = \mu - \frac{1}{2a^i}\sigma^2$. Moreover, investors may disagree upon the first two moments of the distribution of gross returns. Each belief $(\bar{q}^i, V^i)$ is *non-rational* and subjective as it may differ from the *correct* first and second moment of $\tilde{q}$. For the exogenously given market portfolio $x_\mathrm{m} \in \mathbb{R}^n_+$, the CAPM equilibrium in the presence of the short-sale constraint is defined in the following.

Definition 3. *A CAPM equilibrium subject to the short-sale constraint* (1.3) *consists of a price vector* $p_{*c} \in \mathbb{R}^n$ *and portfolio allocations* $x^i_{*c}, \ldots, x^I_{*c} \in \mathbb{R}^n$ *of risky assets such that the following holds:*

1. *Each* x^i_{*c}, $i, \ldots, I$ *is individually constrained-optimal, that is, it solves the utility maximisation problem*

$$\max_{x \in X} \left\{ R_f w_0^i + \langle \pi^i_{*c}, x \rangle - \frac{1}{2a^i} \langle x, V^i x \rangle \right\} \tag{2.1}$$

where $\pi^i_{*c} = \bar{q}^i - R_f p_{*c}$ *is the expected equilibrium excess return of investor* i.

2. *The allocation is feasible, that is, it satisfies the market clearing condition in the market for risky assets*

$$\sum_{i=1}^{I} x^i_{*c} = x_{\mathrm{m}}, \tag{2.2}$$

where $x_{\mathrm{m}} \in \mathbb{R}^n_+$ *is the market portfolio.*

The CAPM equilibrium (2.2) rests upon the market-clearing condition that aggregate demand must equal aggregate supply. Aggregate demand is the sum of all individual demands. Aggregate supply is defined as the theoretical ensemble of securities which, when viewed as the portfolio of all available assets, forms the market portfolio. Each asset in x_{m} is supposed to be in non-zero supply, that is $x_{\mathrm{m}}^{(k)} > 0$ for all $k = 1, \dots, n$.

Assuming linear mean-variance preferences, investor i's *individual asset demand* takes the form

$$\phi^i_c(p; \bar{q}^i, V^i) = \begin{cases} a^i (V^i)^{-1}(\bar{q}^i - R_f p) & \text{if } a^i \langle e_n, (V^i)^{-1}(\bar{q}^i - R_f p)\rangle \geq \chi, \\ a^i W^i(\bar{q}^i - R_f p) + x^i_\chi & \text{otherwise,} \end{cases} \tag{2.3}$$

where $x^i_\chi = \frac{\chi}{\langle e_n, (V^i)^{-1} e_n\rangle}(V^i)^{-1} e_n$. Thus, the market clearing condition reads

$$\Phi_c(p; (\bar{q}^i, V^i)_{i=1}^I) := \sum_{i=1}^{I} \phi^i_c(p; \bar{q}^i, V^i) = x_{\mathrm{m}}, \tag{2.4}$$

and is illustrated in Figure 2.1 for the case $n = 1$. From Figure 2.1(a) we see that investor 1 is short in the classical case of unrestricted short-selling. Figure 2.1(b) depicts the market clearing condition in presence of prohibited short-selling. It reveals that the aggregate demand function Φ_c, is the sum of 2 piecewise affine linear decreasing functions. This example illustrates that in the presence of the short-sale constraint the aggregate demand increases. Consequently, as predicted by MILLER (1977), the asset becomes more expensive. In the remainder of this section we restrict attention to the case of multiple assets.

2.1 Existence and uniqueness

Following WENZELBURGER (2004) and BÖHM AND CHIARELLA (2005), we recall the market-clearing price vector on a frictionless security market with heterogeneous investors.

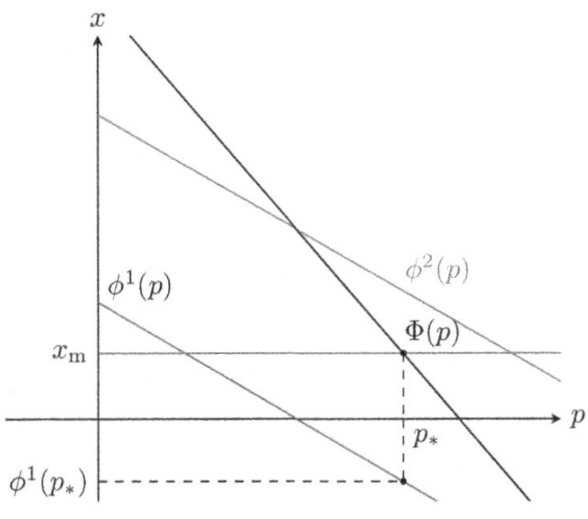

(a) Unconstrained short-selling

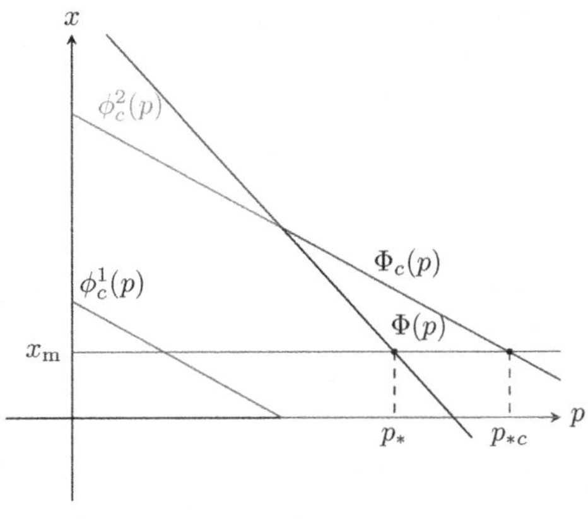

(b) Constrained short-selling

Figure 2.1: Single risky-asset case

Proposition 3. *Consider a financial market with I investors as above. Each investor i is characterised by linear mean-variance preferences and subjective beliefs $(\bar{q}^i, V^i)$. Then, a unique CAPM equilibrium exists and is given by*

$$p_* = \frac{1}{R_f}\left(\sum_{i=1}^{I} A^i \bar{q}^i - A x_\mathrm{m}\right) \quad x_*^j = \sum_{i=1}^{I} B^{ij}(\bar{q}^j - \bar{q}^i) + B^j x_\mathrm{m}, \quad j = 1, \ldots, I, \tag{2.5}$$

with

$$A := \left(\sum_{i=1}^{I} a^i (V^i)^{-1}\right)^{-1} \quad \text{and} \quad A^i := a^i A (V^i)^{-1}, \quad i = 1, \ldots, I \tag{2.6}$$

$$B^j := \left(\sum_{i=1}^{I} \frac{a^i}{a^j} (V^i)^{-1} V^j\right)^{-1} \quad \text{and} \quad B^{ij} := a^i B^j (V^i)^{-1}, \quad i, j = 1, \ldots, I. \tag{2.7}$$

If short-selling is allowed, the existence and uniqueness of an equilibrium price vector follows from the positive definiteness of the matrix A. In the following we show that a unique market clearing price vector in the presence of short-sale constraints exists as well.

Theorem 5. *Consider a financial market with I investors as above. Each investor i is characterised by linear mean-variance preferences and subjective beliefs $(\bar{q}^i, V^i)$. Then, for any $\chi \leq 0$, a CAPM equilibrium in the presence of the short-sale constraint exists and is uniquely determined.*

A formal proof of Theorem 5 is carried out in Appendix A.1. The theorem guarantees that for any number of heterogeneous investors and any short-selling threshold $\chi \leq 0$, the market clearing price vector is uniquely determined. However, the theorem does not make any assertion about the form of the equilibrium prices. Nevertheless, in order to analyse the asset price deviation, we are in need of an explicit form.

In the following we will show that equilibrium prices in the presence of the short-sale constraint can be characterised explicitly if two investors participate in the market of risky assets. This is in line with ANUFRIEV AND TUINSTRA (2013), who derived an explicit characterisation only for the case of investors with two belief types. However, the authors analysed a more simplified model, considering solely one risky asset.

2.2 The case with two investors

Considering a frictionless asset market with two heterogeneous investors, Proposition 3 implies that the equilibrium price vector is given by

$$p_* = \frac{1}{R_f}\left(a^1(V^1)^{-1} + a^2(V^2)^{-1}\right)^{-1}\left(a^1(V^1)^{-1}\bar{q}^1 + a^2(V^2)^{-1}\bar{q}^2 - x_{\mathrm{m}}\right), \quad (2.8)$$

hereafter referred to as the *unconstrained* equilibrium price vector. Before we derive the equilibrium asset prices on the regulated market, we note that only the following three cases can occur:

1. Both investors fulfil the short-sale constraint at the *unconstrained* equilibrium price vector p_*, i.e.

$$\langle e_n, x_*^i\rangle = a^i\langle e_n, (V^i)^{-1}(\bar{q}^i - R_f p_*)\rangle \geq \chi \quad \text{for all} \quad i = 1, 2;$$

2. Investor 1 violates the short-sale constraint at prices p_*, i.e.

$$\langle e_n, x_*^1\rangle = a^1\langle e_n, (V^1)^{-1}(\bar{q}^1 - R_f p_*)\rangle < \chi;$$

3. Investor 2 violates the short-sale constraint at prices p_*, i.e.

$$\langle e_n, x_*^2\rangle = a^2\langle e_n, (V^2)^{-1}(\bar{q}^2 - R_f p_*)\rangle < \chi.$$

Note that, the case in which both investors violate the short-sale constraint at prices p_* is not possible as it would violate the market clearing condition

$$\langle e_n, x_*^1 + x_*^2\rangle = \langle e_n, x_{\mathrm{m}}\rangle > 0.$$

If case 1 occurs, the portfolio allocation is optimal and the price vector p_* clears the regulated market. Consequently, the short-sale constraint does not affect equilibrium prices. In the other cases the short-sale constraint becomes binding and the short-seller will restructure her portfolio. The corresponding market clearing price vector will thus differ from p_*. Assuming the short-seller to be investor 1, the corresponding market clearing condition reads

$$a^1 W^1(\bar{q}^1 - R_f p) + x_\chi^1 + a^2 (V^2)^{-1}(\bar{q}^2 - R_f p) = x_{\mathrm{m}}. \tag{2.9}$$

The solution of (2.9) is given by the price vector

$$p_c^1 = \frac{1}{R_f}\left(\sum_{i=1}^{2} A_c^i \bar{q}^i - A_c\left(x_{\mathrm{m}} - x_\chi^1\right)\right) \tag{2.10}$$

where

$$A_c := \left(a^1 W^1 + a^2 (V^2)^{-1}\right)^{-1} \quad \text{and} \quad A_c^i := \begin{cases} a^1 A_c W^1 & \text{if } i = 1, \\ a^2 A_c (V^2)^{-1} & \text{if } i = 2. \end{cases} \tag{2.11}$$

Notice that $\left(a^1 W^1 + a^2 (V^2)^{-1}\right)^{-1}$ exists since $a^1 W^1 + a^2 (V^2)^{-1}$ is positive definite. Using the same reasoning, the corresponding price vector of investor 2 being the short-seller at prices p_*, is given by

$$p_c^2 = \frac{1}{R_f}\left(\sum_{i=1}^{2} \hat{A}_c^i \bar{q}^i - \hat{A}_c\left(x_{\mathrm{m}} - x_\chi^2\right)\right) \tag{2.12}$$

where

$$\hat{A}_c := \left(a^1 (V^1)^{-1} + a^2 W^2\right)^{-1} \quad \text{and} \quad \hat{A}_c^i := \begin{cases} a^1 \hat{A}_c (V^1)^{-1} & \text{if } i = 1, \\ a^2 \hat{A}_c W^2 & \text{if } i = 2. \end{cases} \tag{2.13}$$

These results are summarised in the following theorem.

Theorem 6. *Consider a financial market with 2 investors. Each investor i is characterised by linear mean-variance preferences and subjective beliefs $(\bar{q}^i, V^i)$. Let p_c^1 and p_c^2 be defined as in (2.10) and (2.12), respectively. Then, for any $\chi \le 0$, a unique market clearing price vector exists and is given by*

$$p_{*c} = \begin{cases} p_* & \text{if } a^i \langle e_n, (V^i)^{-1}(\bar{q}^i - R_f p_*)\rangle \ge \chi \quad \text{for } i = 1, 2, \\ p_c^i & \text{if } a^i \langle e_n, (V^i)^{-1}(\bar{q}^i - R_f p_*)\rangle < \chi. \end{cases} \tag{2.14}$$

The pricing formula (2.14) indicates that the *constrained-market clearing* price vector p_{*c} is determined by the diversity of beliefs but however, does not necessary reveal all of the private information that investors have. Theorem 6 does not require investors to have common knowledge about the other investor's wealth or utility functions as well as beliefs about the first two moments.

At the market clearing prices p_{*c}, both investors will hold optimal portfolios which satisfy the short-sale constraint. For the sake of simplicity, we assume without loss of generality, that investors' beliefs are such that investor 1 is the short-seller at prices p_*.

Assumption 4. *Let $(\bar{q}^1, V^1) \neq (\bar{q}^2, V^2)$ be the beliefs of investors 1 and 2, respectively. The expectations $(\bar{q}^i, V^i)$, $i = 1, 2$ are considered to be such that*

$$a^1 \langle e_n, (V^1)^{-1}(\bar{q}^1 - R_f p_*)\rangle < \chi,$$

so that investor 1 violates the short-sale constraint in the unconstrained equilibrium.

Assumption 4 ensures that the constrained-market clearing price vector is given by $p_{*c} = p_c^1$.

Theorem 7. *Let the hypothesis of Assumption 4 be satisfied and consider a financial market with 2 investors. Each investor i is characterised by linear mean-variance preferences and subjective beliefs $(\bar{q}^i, V^i)$. Then for any $\chi \leq 0$, a unique CAPM equilibrium in the presence of the short-sale constraint exists and is given by the price vector*

$$p_{*c} = \frac{1}{R_f}\left(\sum_{i=1}^{2} A_c^i \bar{q}^i - A_c\left(x_{\mathrm{m}} - x_\chi^1\right)\right)$$

and portfolio allocations

$$x_{*c}^1 = B_c^{21}(\bar{q}^1 - \bar{q}^2) + B_c^1(x_{\mathrm{m}} - x_\chi^1) + x_\chi^1 \tag{2.15}$$

$$x_{*c}^2 = B_c^{12}(\bar{q}^2 - \bar{q}^1) + B_c^2(x_{\mathrm{m}} - x_\chi^1), \tag{2.16}$$

with

$$B_c^j := \begin{cases} a^1 W^1 A_c & \text{if } j = 1, \\ a^2 (V^2)^{-1} A_c & \text{if } j = 2, \end{cases}$$

and

$$B_c^{21} := a^2 B_c^1 (V^2)^{-1}$$
$$B_c^{12} := a^1 B_c^2 W^1.$$

where the matrices A_c and A_c^i are defined as in (2.11).

The matrices B_c^j, B_c^{21} and B_c^{12} are well-defined for both investors $j \in \{1, 2\}$. The coefficient matrices B_c^1 and B_c^{21} of the short-seller, however, have zero entries in the n-th row and column and are thus singular. Consequently, $\langle e_n, x^1_{*c}\rangle = \langle e_n, x^1_\chi\rangle = \chi$ and due to the market clearing condition, $\langle e_n, x^2_{*c}\rangle = \langle e_n, x_{\mathrm{m}}\rangle - \chi$. In other words, at prices p_{*c}, the short-seller is restricted to borrow χ shares of asset n, whereas the long-seller takes a long position of $x^{(n)}_{\mathrm{m}} - \chi$ shares.

As discussed in the introduction of this section, JARROW (1980) disproved the overpricing hypothesis of MILLER (1977) and HARRISON AND KREPS (1978) by means of a counterexample. Nevertheless, the author did not provide a necessary and sufficient criterion indicating whether or not equilibrium asset prices fall. Such a criterion is established in the next theorem.

Theorem 8. *Let the hypothesis of Assumption 4 be satisfied. Then the deviation of the constrained equilibrium prices from the unconstrained prices p_* is given by*

$$p_{*c} - p_* = \underbrace{\frac{1}{R_f}\frac{\chi - \langle e_n, \phi^1(p_*)\rangle}{\langle e_n, (V^1)^{-1}e_n\rangle}}_{\geq 0} A_c(V^1)^{-1}e_n, \tag{2.17}$$

where $\phi^1(p_*) = a^1(V^1)^{-1}(\bar{q}^1 - R_f p_*)$ is the short-seller's individual asset demand at the equilibrium price p_*. In particular, the price of the k-th asset will increase due to a binding short-sale constraint if and only if

$$\langle e_k, A_c(V^1)^{-1}e_n\rangle = \langle e_k, (a^1W^1 + a^2(V^2)^{-1})^{-1}(V^1)^{-1}e_n\rangle \geq 0. \tag{2.18}$$

Theorem 8 extends Jarrow's results showing that overpricing of equilibrium asset prices is solely attributable to the investors' second moments of the gross return distribution. Equation (2.18) formalises the *substitution effect* established by JARROW (1980): a decline in aggregate demand can result because of a decline in the demand of substitute securities leading to underpricing. The k-th entry in the vector $A_c(V^1)^{-1}e_n$ detects over- or underpricing of asset k. The hypothesised overpricing in the simplified single-asset model directly follows from Equation (2.18) as $A_c(V^1)^{-1} \in \mathbb{R}$ is a positive scalar and given by

$$A_c(V^1)^{-1} = \frac{1}{a^2}\frac{\mathbb{V}\mathrm{ar}^2(\tilde{q})}{\mathbb{V}\mathrm{ar}^1(\tilde{q})} > 0.$$

The gap $\chi - \langle e_n, \phi^1(p_*)\rangle$ in Equation (2.17) measures how far off from the unconstrained optimum the short-selling threshold is set. Theorem 8 implies that this gap cannot cause but only can amplify overpricing or underpricing. In particular, we conclude that the first moments $\bar{q}^1$, $\bar{q}^2$ influence the magnitude of over- or underpricing but do not induce these effects. To the best of our knowledge, a deviation formula (2.17) for an arbitrary but finite number of assets and arbitrary covariance matrices is so far missing. The proof is listed in Appendix A.1. We illustrate Theorem 8 by means of the two-asset case.

Example 7. *Consider a financial market with two risky assets, one risk-free bond and two investors with risk-tolerances a^i, $i = 1, 2$. If Assumption 4 is satisfied the vector $A_c(V^1)^{-1}e_2$ can be written as*

$$\kappa \begin{pmatrix} \mathbb{C}\text{ov}^2\mathbb{V}\text{ar}^1\left(\tilde{q}^{(1)}\right) - \mathbb{C}\text{ov}^1\mathbb{V}\text{ar}^2\left(\tilde{q}^{(1)}\right) \\ \frac{a^1}{a^2}\det V^2 + \mathbb{V}\text{ar}^1\left(\tilde{q}^{(1)}\right)\mathbb{V}\text{ar}^2\left(\tilde{q}^{(2)}\right) - \mathbb{C}\text{ov}^2\mathbb{C}\text{ov}^1 \end{pmatrix},$$

where κ is defined as

$$\kappa := \frac{\mathbb{V}\text{ar}^1\left(\tilde{q}^{(1)}\right)}{\det V^1\left(a^2\mathbb{V}\text{ar}^1\left(\tilde{q}^{(1)}\right) + a^1\mathbb{V}\text{ar}^2\left(\tilde{q}^{(1)}\right)\right)} > 0,$$

and $\mathbb{C}\text{ov}^i = \mathbb{C}\text{ov}^i\left(\tilde{q}^{(1)}, \tilde{q}^{(2)}\right)$ for $i = 1, 2$ is the covariance estimated by investor i. Thus, the price of (the unregulated) asset 1 will increase if and only if

$$\mathbb{C}\text{ov}^2\mathbb{V}\text{ar}^1\left(\tilde{q}^{(1)}\right) > \mathbb{C}\text{ov}^1\mathbb{V}\text{ar}^2\left(\tilde{q}^{(1)}\right). \tag{2.19}$$

The price of the regulated asset will increase if and only if

$$\frac{a^1}{a^2}\det V^2 + \mathbb{V}\text{ar}^1\left(\tilde{q}^{(1)}\right)\mathbb{V}\text{ar}^2\left(\tilde{q}^{(2)}\right) > \mathbb{C}\text{ov}^2\mathbb{C}\text{ov}^1. \tag{2.20}$$

Inequality (2.19) is fulfilled whenever the long-seller (investor 2) expects a positive and the short-seller a negative correlation between the risky assets, that is if $\mathbb{C}\text{ov}^2 > 0$ and $\mathbb{C}\text{ov}^1 \leq 0$. On the other hand, if $\mathbb{C}\text{ov}^2 \leq 0$ and $\mathbb{C}\text{ov}^1 > 0$, the price of asset 1 will decrease. Considering the regulated asset, we see that the left hand side of (2.20) is positive. Therefore, adverse estimates about the correlation of risky assets, i.e. $\mathbb{C}\text{ov}^2\mathbb{C}\text{ov}^1 < 0$, imply an increase of the equilibrium price of the regulated asset. The next lemma studies the case in which the investors' correlations are aligned so that $\mathbb{C}\text{ov}^1\mathbb{C}\text{ov}^2 \geq 0$.

Lemma 4. *Let the hypothesis of Assumption 4 be satisfied and $n = 2$. Then the following holds true:*

1. *Let $\mathbb{C}\text{ov}^1 \geq 0$ and $\mathbb{C}\text{ov}^2 > 0$. Then, if the price of asset 1 increases, the price of asset 2 will increase as well.*

2. *Let $\mathbb{C}\text{ov}^1 \leq 0$ and $\mathbb{C}\text{ov}^2 < 0$. Then, if the price of asset 1 decreases, the price of asset 2 will increase as well.*

The next proposition is a direct consequence of Theorem 8 and analyses the deviation of equilibrium prices in case of n risky assets.

Proposition 4. *Let the hypothesis of Assumption 4 be satisfied. Then the following holds true:*

1. *If* $V^1 = \gamma V^2$ *for some* $\gamma \in \mathbb{R}_+$ *then* $p_{*c} - p_* = (0, \ldots, 0, \delta)^\top$, *where*

$$\delta = \frac{1}{R_f} \frac{\chi - \langle e_n, \phi^1(p_*)\rangle}{\langle e_n, (V^1)^{-1} e_n\rangle} \frac{1}{a^2\gamma} > 0.$$

2. *If* $\mathrm{Cov}^i\left(\tilde{q}^{(k)}, \tilde{q}^{(n)}\right) = 0$ *for all assets* $k \in \{1, \ldots n-1\}$ *and both investors* $i = 1, 2$, *then* $p_{*c} - p_* = (0, \ldots, 0, \zeta)^\top$, *where*

$$\zeta = \frac{1}{R_f} \frac{\chi - \langle e_n, \phi^1(p_*)\rangle}{\mathrm{Var}^2(\tilde{q}^{(n)})} > 0.$$

.

In particular, in both cases, the following holds true:

$$p_{*c}^{(k)} = p_*^{(k)} \quad \text{for all} \quad k \neq n \quad \text{and} \quad p_{*c}^{(n)} > p_*^{(n)}.$$

Assuming that investors agree on the same covariance matrix, JARROW (1980) showed that the equilibrium asset price of the regulated security will always rise in the presence of the short-sale constraint. Proposition 4 relaxes this assumption: overpricing will also occur if the covariance matrices differ by a positive factor. Another well-known condition for overpricing is the case of heterogeneous but diagonal covariance matrices, so that *all* risky assets are pairwise uncorrelated. Also this assumption is relaxed by Proposition 4.

A common hypothesis alongside the overpricing theory is that a more stringent regulation in terms of a larger short-selling threshold χ (i.e. smaller $|\chi|$) amplifies overpricing.[4] From Theorem 8 we observe that, ceteris paribus, the price deviation $p_{*c} - p_*$ is (linearly) increasing in χ. Therefore, a larger short-selling threshold can indeed amplify overpricing. However, if investors' beliefs are such that underpricing occurs, a larger χ will distort asset prices even further downward. Summarising, a stringent regulation alone cannot induce overpricing or underpricing but amplify both.

So far, we considered a financial market with two heterogeneous investors. In the following section we investigate the case of more than 2 investors and the associated difficulties.

2.3 The case with three and more investors

The existence and uniqueness of a market clearing price vector for a finite number of investors is guaranteed by Theorem 5. Its form, however, cannot be determined without use of an algorithmic procedure.

[4] In ANUFRIEV AND TUINSTRA (2013), stringent regulation was modelled by larger trading costs on short-sales.

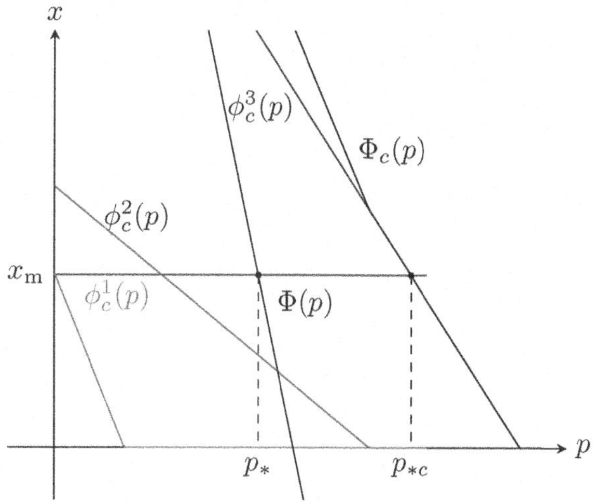

Figure 2.2: The case of 3 investors

In the case of two investors, the long-seller at prices p_* holds a mean-variance efficient portfolio at prices p_{*c} as well (see Figure 2.1). If, however, more than 2 investors participate in the financial market, the long-seller at prices p_* may be restricted to hold a constrained-efficient portfolio at prices p_{*c}. This scenario is illustrated in Figure 2.2 with the single-asset case. We see that investor 2 is restricted to a zero-position at price p_{*c}, despite being a long-seller at prices p_*. In other words, *ex-ante*, i.e. at prices p_*, it is not possible to indicate investors who hold constrained-efficient portfolios at prices p_{*c}. This property, however, is needed to determine the form of the market clearing price vector in the presence of the short-sale constraint.

A brute-force method of computing all possible market clearing price vectors and verifying (constrained-)optimality of portfolio allocations is a computational challenge. The pricing formula (2.14) for $I = 2$ consists of 3 price vectors. With increasing number of investors, however, this number rises exponentially. For $I = 3$, there are 7 possible price vectors in total: if at prices p_* all investors satisfy the short-sale constraint, the equilibrium prices vector remains unaffected, i.e. $p_{*c} = p_*$. If only one investor is violating the short-sale constraint 3 cases are possible. Finally, if two investors violate the short-sale constraint, there are 3 possible cases as well. For I investors the price selection consists of

$$\sum_{i=0}^{I-1} \binom{I}{i} = 2^I - 1 \tag{2.21}$$

different prices. The expression $\binom{I}{i}$ denotes the binomial coefficient and expresses the number of prices when i investors out of I hold a short position at the equilibrium prices p_*. If $I = 100$ investors participate in the financial market, the price selection (2.14) consists of more than 10^{30} different prices.

The study carried out in this section analysed the effects of short-sale constraints on equilibrium prices in a static setting. The next chapter embeds the model into a dynamical framework and seeks to analyse how the presence of a short-sale constraint affects the *long-run* behaviour of asset prices and allocations.

3 Dynamic Model

To examine the consequences of short-sale constraints on asset prices in the long-run is of particular importance both from a political as well as academic point of view. Most of the models in financial literature pursuing this question, however, consider a single-asset market or assume that investors are fully rational. To this end, the present chapter investigates asset price and allocation dynamics on a financial market with multiple assets and heterogeneous investors, including noise traders.[1] The key idea is to extend the static two-period model of the previous chapter to a dynamic model by linking together an infinite series of two-period economies. While in the previous chapter the formation of investors' beliefs was exogenous, this chapter allows re-evaluation of expectations based on past forecast errors. In this framework, a numerical case study of asset price and allocation dynamics is presented. The numerical experiments aim to analyse the applicability of the short-sale constraint as an instrument to stabilise financial markets. More specifically, we want to answer the following two questions:

1. Does limited short-selling prevent a market decline by causing overvaluation of asset prices?

2. Is the price process less volatile in the presence of the short-sale constraint?

The presented model differs from comparable dynamical models in three ways. Firstly, considering a financial market with multiple risky assets, we find out that short-sale constraints have mixed effects on prices. Single-asset models like in Anufriev and Tuinstra (2013) and Dercole and Radi (2014), on the other hand, observe a systematic overvaluation of the regulated security. A second substantial difference is the existence of investors whose portfolio decisions are not captured by a standard microeconomic decision model. These investors are called *noise traders* and their interaction in the presence

[1] A comprehensive survey of the literature on asset-price dynamics with unrestricted short-selling is Hens and Schenk-Hoppé (2009).

G. Hunanyan, *The Consequences of Short-Sale Constraints on the Stability of Financial Markets*, Finanzwirtschaft, Banken und Bankmanagement | Finance, Banks and Bank Management, https://doi.org/10.1007/978-3-658-27956-1_4

of the short-sale constraint can distort equilibrium asset prices upwards as well as downwards. Finally, a third novelty is the heterogeneity of investors' second moments.[2]

This chapter is structured as follows: Section 3.1 embeds the static model of the previous chapter into the framework of dynamical systems theory. While the concept of a temporary equilibrium is used to model the basic market mechanism of a financial market, forecasting rules stipulate the way in which investors re-evaluate expectations. Section 3.2 presents a numerical simulation study in which all model parameters but the investors' second moments are kept fixed. Section 3.3 examines the consequences of short-sale constraints on the price volatility.

3.1 Prerequisites

Following WENZELBURGER (2009), we consider a financial market containing $n+1$ financial instruments. The risk-free bond y pays constant return $R_f = 1+r_f > 0$ per unit invested in the previous period. The bond price is normalised to 1. The other $k = 1, \ldots, n$ financial instruments are risky shares of n firms that are traded at prices $p_t = \left(p_t^{(1)}, \ldots, p_t^{(n)}\right)$ of the discrete time period $t \in \mathbb{N}$. It is assumed that investment decisions take place *prior* to trading. Shareholders of firm k in period t receive a *stochastic* dividend payment of $d_t^{(k)}$ per unit of share, such that the vector of all dividend payments in period t is given by

$$d_t = \left(d_t^{(1)}, \ldots, d_t^{(n)}\right) \in \mathbb{R}_+^n. \tag{3.1}$$

For given prices p_{t+1}, the stochastic gross returns of period $t+1$ are cum-dividend prices

$$q_{t+1} = p_{t+1} + d_{t+1}. \tag{3.2}$$

In this asset market, two investors $i = 1, 2$ with linear mean-variance preferences with heterogeneous and subjective beliefs $(\bar{q}_t^i, V_t^i)$ interact. At the initial state $t = 0$ both investors $i = 1, 2$ receive an endowment w_0^i denominated in a consumption good. As in the static model, we suppose that consumption does not take place and the investors' planning horizon consists of one period. In addition to the two investors, we assume that in each period t a group of traders, whose portfolio decisions are not captured by a standard microeconomic decision problem, is active in the asset market. The aggregate portfolio holdings of these so-called *noise traders* is given by a

[2] Restricting our attention to the case of homogeneous second moment beliefs, we obtain the overpricing of the regulated security as a special case.

stochastic share $\xi_t \in \mathbb{R}^n$ of risky assets. The probabilistic prerequisites on the exogenous dividend process and noise process are given in the following assumption.

Assumption 5. *Let $(\Omega, \mathcal{F}, \mathbb{P})$ be a probability space and $\{\mathcal{F}_t\}_{t\in\mathbb{N}}$ an increasing stochastic process of sub-σ-algebras of $\mathcal{F}$.*

1. *The dividend payments are described by a $\{\mathcal{F}_t\}_{t\in\mathbb{N}}$-adapted stochastic process $\{d_t\}_{t\in\mathbb{N}}$ on $(\Omega, \mathcal{F}, \mathbb{P})$ with values in $\mathbb{D} \subset \mathbb{R}^n_+$.*
2. *Noise traders' transactions are described by a $\{\mathcal{F}_t\}_{t\in\mathbb{N}}$-adapted stochastic process $\{\xi_t\}_{t\in\mathbb{N}}$ on $(\Omega, \mathcal{F}, \mathbb{P})$ with values in $\mathbb{R}^n$ which is uncorrelated with the dividend process defined in 1.*

For simplicity, we assume that the exogenous dividend process is known. From the perspective of investor i who, at time $t-1$, owns a portfolio of risky assets $x^i_{t-1} \in \mathbb{R}^n$ and bonds $y^i_{t-1} \in \mathbb{R}$, the period-t wealth can be written as

$$w^i_t = R_f y^i_{t-1} + \langle (p_t + d_t), x^i_{t-1} \rangle. \tag{3.3}$$

The period-t budget constraint for a new portfolio (x, y)[3] in turn reads

$$w^i_t = \langle p_t, x \rangle + y.$$

Let the price vector p_t, which is only known *after trading* in period t, be given. Then, investor i's period-$t+1$ wealth associated with (x, y) becomes

$$\begin{aligned} w^i_{t+1} &= R_f y + \langle q_{t+1}, x \rangle \\ &= R_f (w^i_t - \langle p_t, x \rangle) + \langle q_{t+1}, x \rangle \\ &= R_f w^i_t + \langle q_{t+1} - R_f p_t, x \rangle. \end{aligned}$$

Let $\bar{q}^i_t := \mathbb{E}^i_t[q_{t+1}]$ denote the expected cum-dividend price conditional on information available at date t. Setting $\pi^i_t := \mathbb{E}^i_t[q_{t+1}] - R_f p_t$ as the *vector of subjectively expected excess returns*, the *subjectively expected future wealth* of investor $i = 1, 2$ associated with portfolio (x, y) can be written as

$$\mathbb{E}^i_t[w^i_{t+1}] = R_f w^i_t + \langle \pi^i_t, x \rangle, \tag{3.4}$$

whereas the *subjectively perceived standard deviation of future wealth* is

$$\sqrt{\mathrm{Var}^i_t[w^i_{t+1}]} = \sqrt{\langle x, V^i_t x \rangle}. \tag{3.5}$$

[3] Common notation is to use super- and subscripts in order to differentiate the variable from its realisation. Therefore x denotes the variable whereas, x^i_t is referred to the portfolio holding of investor i at time $t \geq 0$.

Setting

$$\mathrm{M}(x; w_t^i, \pi_t^i) := R_f w_t^i + \langle \pi_t^i, x\rangle \quad \text{and} \quad \mathrm{Sd}\left(x; V_t^i\right) := \sqrt{\langle x, V_t^i x\rangle},$$

the decision problem of investor i in the presence of the short-sale constraint becomes

$$\max_{x\in\mathbb{R}^n}\left\{\mathrm{M}(x; w_t^i, \pi_t^i) - \frac{1}{2a^i}\mathrm{Sd}^2(x; V_t^i)\right\} \quad \text{s.t.} \quad \langle e_n, x\rangle \geq \chi, \tag{3.6}$$

where a^i, denotes the risk tolerance of investor $i \in \{1, 2\}$.

Assuming linear mean-variance preferences, investor i's individual asset demand in the static model was given by

$$x_c^i = \begin{cases} a^i(V^i)^{-1}(\bar{q}^i - R_f p) & \text{if } a^i\langle e_n, (V^i)^{-1}(\bar{q}^i - R_f p)\rangle \geq \chi, \\ a^i W^i(\bar{q}^i - R_f p) + x_\chi^i & \text{otherwise,} \end{cases} \tag{3.7}$$

where $x_\chi^i = \frac{\chi}{\langle e_n, (V^i)^{-1} e_n\rangle}(V^i)^{-1} e_n$.

By introducing the time index t into Equation (3.7), the gross-demand of risky assets of an investor i with beliefs $(\bar{q}_t^i, V_t^i)$ becomes $x_{c,t}^i = \phi_c^i\left(p; \bar{q}_t^i, V_t^i\right)$ where

$$\phi_c^i\left(p; \bar{q}_t^i, V_t^i\right) = \begin{cases} a^i(V_t^i)^{-1}(\bar{q}_t^i - R_f p) & \text{if } a^i\langle e_n, (V_t^i)^{-1}(\bar{q}_t^i - R_f p)\rangle \geq \chi, \\ a^i W_t^i(\bar{q}_t^i - R_f p) + x_{\chi,t}^i & \text{otherwise,} \end{cases} \tag{3.8}$$

and $x_{\chi,t}^i := \frac{\chi}{\langle e_n, (V_t^i)^{-1} e_n\rangle}(V_t^i)^{-1} e_n$.

In order to extend the two-period model to a multi-period one we reinterpret the static equilibrium (3.8) as a *temporary equilibrium* and endogenise the formation of the investors' beliefs in a second step. In other words, by specifying forecasting rules, we allow re-evaluation of expectations based on past forecasting errors. For the exogenously given market portfolio $x_{\mathrm{m}} \in \mathbb{R}^n$, the temporary CAPM equilibrium in the presence of the short-sale constraint is defined as follows.

Definition 4. A temporary CAPM equilibrium *in period t consists of a price vector $p_{c,t} \in \mathbb{R}^n$ and portfolio allocations $x_{c,t}^i \in \mathbb{R}^n$, $i = 1, 2$ of risky assets such that the following holds:*

1. *Each $x_{c,t}^i$, $i = 1, 2$ is individually constrained-optimal, i.e. solves the utility maximisation problem* (3.6).

2. *The allocation is feasible, that is, it satisfies the market clearing condition in the market for risky assets*

$$\sum_{i=1}^{2} x_{c,t}^{i} + \xi_t = x_{\mathrm{m}}, \tag{3.9}$$

where $x_{\mathrm{m}} \in \mathbb{R}_{+}^{n}$ is the market portfolio.

Denoting investor i's *net-demand* of risky assets by $x_{c,t}^{i} - x_{c,t-1}^{i}$, the market clearing condition of the asset market in period t reads,

$$\sum_{i=1}^{2} \left[\phi_c^i\left(p; \bar{q}_t^i, V_t^i\right) - x_{c,t-1}^{i}\right] + \xi_t - \xi_{t-1} = 0, \tag{3.10}$$

where $\xi_t \in \mathbb{R}^n$ refers to the portfolio holdings of the noise traders after trading in period t. Since aggregate demand of the previous period equals aggregate supply $x_{\mathrm{m}} \in \mathbb{R}_{+}^{n}$, i.e.

$$\sum_{i=1}^{2} x_{c,t-1}^{i} + \xi_{t-1} = x_{\mathrm{m}},$$

the market clearing condition (3.10) transforms to,

$$\sum_{i=1}^{2} \phi_c^i\left(p; \bar{q}_t^i, V_t^i\right) + \xi_t = x_{\mathrm{m}}. \tag{3.11}$$

In case that short-selling is permitted, WENZELBURGER (2009) showed that a CAPM equilibrium with heterogeneous beliefs $(\bar{q}_t^i, V_t^i)_{i=1}^{2}$, is given by

$$p_t = G\left(\xi_t, (\bar{q}_t^i, V_t^i)_{i=1}^{2}\right) := \frac{1}{R_f}\left(\sum_{i=1}^{2} A_t^i \bar{q}_t^i - A_t(x_{\mathrm{m}} - \xi_t)\right), \tag{3.12}$$

$$x_t^i = \phi^i\left(p_t; \bar{q}_t^i, V_t^i\right) := \sum_{j=1}^{2} B_t^{ji}(\bar{q}_t^i - \bar{q}_t^j) + B_t^i(x_{\mathrm{m}} - \xi_t), \quad i = 1, 2, \tag{3.13}$$

where

$$A_t := \left(\sum_{i=1}^{2} a^i (V_t^i)^{-1}\right)^{-1} \quad \text{and} \quad A_t^i := a_t^i A_t (V_t^i)^{-1}, \quad i = 1, 2 \tag{3.14}$$

$$B_t^i := \left(\sum_{j=1}^{2} \frac{a^j}{a^i} (V_t^j)^{-1} V_t^i\right)^{-1} \quad \text{and} \quad B_t^{ji} := a^j B_t^i (V_t^j)^{-1}, \quad i, j = 1, 2. \tag{3.15}$$

If, based on heterogeneous beliefs $(\bar{q}_t^i, V_t^i)_{i=1}^2$, the temporary equilibrium allocation x_t^i in period t satisfies

$$\langle e_n, x_t^i \rangle = \sum_{j=1}^{2} \langle e_n, B_t^{ji}(\bar{q}_t^i - \bar{q}_t^j) \rangle + \langle e_n, B_t^i(x_{\rm m} - \xi_t) \rangle \geq \chi \quad \text{for} \quad i = 1, 2,$$

Equations (3.12) and (3.13) also define a temporary CAPM equilibrium on the regulated financial market. If, however, the short-sale constraint is violated by one of the investor's equilibrium allocation, the above equations do not define a CAPM equilibrium on the asset market with constrained short-selling. Suppose, without loss of generality, that in period t investor 1 is the short-seller at the equilibrium price vector p_t, that is $\langle e_n, x_t^1 \rangle < \chi$. Then for arbitrary beliefs $(\bar{q}_t^i, V_t^i)$, the temporary market equilibrium in the presence of constrained short-selling is given in the following proposition.

Proposition 5. *Consider a regulated financial market with two investors. Each investor is characterised by linear mean-variance preferences and subjective beliefs* $(\bar{q}_t^i, V_t^i)_{i=1}^2$. *Then a unique temporary CAPM equilibrium exists. The* temporary equilibrium map *and the* temporary equilibrium allocations *are given by*

$$p_{c,t} = G_c(\xi_t, (\bar{q}_t^i, V_t^i)_{i=1}^2) := \frac{1}{R_f}\left(\sum_{i=1}^{2} A_{c,t}^i \bar{q}_t^i - A_{c,t}\left(x_{\rm m} - \xi_t - x_{\chi,t}^1\right)\right) \tag{3.16}$$

and

$$\begin{aligned} x_{c,t}^1 &= B_{c,t}^{21}(\bar{q}_t^1 - \bar{q}_t^2) + B_{c,t}^1(x_{\rm m} - \xi_t - x_{\chi,t}^1) + x_{\chi,t}^1 \\ x_{c,t}^2 &= B_{c,t}^{12}(\bar{q}_t^2 - \bar{q}_t^1) + B_{c,t}^2(x_{\rm m} - x_{\chi,t}^1), \end{aligned} \tag{3.17}$$

respectively, where $x_{\chi,t}^1 = \frac{\chi}{\langle e_n, (V_t^1)^{-1} e_n \rangle}(V_t^1)^{-1} e_n$. *The coefficient matrices are given as*

$$A_{c,t} := \left(a^1 W_t^1 + a^2 (V_t^2)^{-1}\right)^{-1} \quad \text{and} \quad A_{c,t}^i := \begin{cases} a^1 A_{c,t} W_t^1 & \text{if } i = 1, \\ a^2 A_{c,t} (V_t^2)^{-1} & \text{if } i = 2, \end{cases}$$

and

$$B_{c,t}^j := \begin{cases} a^1 W_t^1 A_{c,t} & \text{if } j = 1, \\ a^2 (V_t^2)^{-1} A_{c,t} & \text{if } j = 2, \end{cases}$$

and

$$B_{c,t}^{21} := a^2 B_{c,t}^1 (V_t^2)^{-1}, \quad B_{c,t}^{12} := a^1 B_{c,t}^2 W_t^1.$$

The positive definiteness of investor 2's subjective covariance matrix implies that all coefficient matrices are well defined. The map G_c determines the market-clearing prices in each period on a financial market with constrained short-selling. The equilibrium price vector $p_{c,t}$ given in (3.16) is essentially the same as derived in (2.14) except that it accounts for noise traders' transactions.

Note that the economic price law (3.16) does not describe an evolution of asset prices since there is not a priori dependence of beliefs on current asset prices. A complete description of the price process in the form of a dynamical system requires the notion of a *forecasting rule* of beliefs: a procedure according to which investors form and update their beliefs. Following WENZELBURGER (2009), we assume that subjective beliefs $(\bar{q}_t^i, V_t^i)_{i=1}^2$ are set prior to trading in period t, and hence are formed on the basis of information observable up to time $t-1$. We distinguish between *public information*

$$\mathbb{I}_t = \{(p_s, d_s)\}_{s=t-\tau}^{t-1},$$

which is the observable data of prices and dividends up to time t, with τ being the length of the memory and *private information* of investor i

$$\mathbb{I}_t^i = \left\{(\bar{q}_s^i, V_s^i)\right\}_{s=t-\tau}^{t-1},$$

which is unobservable for investor $j \neq i$. The re-evaluation of expectations based on past forecasting errors contains an expectational lead: beliefs are one period ahead of the map G_c with respect to the realisation of prices. This sequential structure is illustrated in Figure 3.1.[4] Formally, the forecasting rule

$t-1$	ξ_{t-1}	t	ξ_t	$t+1$	ξ_{t+1}
$\bar{q}_{t-1}^i$	d_{t-1}	$\bar{q}_t^i$	d_t	$\bar{q}_{t+1}^i$	d_{t+1}
V_{t-1}^i	p_{t-1}	V_t^i	p_t	V_{t+1}^i	p_{t+1}

Figure 3.1: Sequential structure

of investor i, which is based on private and public information for the first and second moments, can be written as

$$\bar{q}_t^i = \Psi_1^i\left(\{p_s, d_s, \bar{q}_s^i, V_s^i\}_{t-\tau}^{t-1}\right)$$

[4] The timeline of price formation is taken from WENZELBURGER (2009).

and

$$V_t^i = \Psi_2^i \left(\{p_s, d_s, \bar{q}_s^i, V_s^i\}_{t-\tau}^{t-1} \right),$$

respectively. Together with the market-clearing price vector (3.16), the constrained-optimal allocation (3.17), as well as a model for the dividend process and for noise traders transaction respectively, we obtain the system

$$\begin{cases} p_{c,t} &= G_c \left(\xi_t, (\bar{q}_t^i, V_t^i)_{i=1}^2 \right), \\ x_{c,t}^i &= \phi_c^i \left(p_{c,t}; \bar{q}_t^i, V_t^i \right), \\ \bar{q}_t^i &= \Psi_1^i \left(\{p_s, d_s, \bar{q}_s^i, V_s^i\}_{t-\tau}^{t-1} \right), \\ V_t^i &= \Psi_2^i \left(\left\{p_s, d_s, \bar{q}_s^i, V_s^i\right\}_{t-\tau}^{t-1} \right), \end{cases} \tag{3.18}$$

of stochastic difference equations describing the evolution of the stock market. There is a great degree of freedom to specify investors' expectations formation Ψ_1 and Ψ_2 a priori. In the remainder of this chapter we restrict attention to investors who form their beliefs based on adaptive expectations, referred to as *chartists*.

3.2 Asset price dynamics

In this section we analyse the dynamics of asset prices and allocations on a financial market in which two chartists and noise traders participate. Chartists use past price series to infer the movement of future price. Therefore, they have subjective beliefs and in general cannot predict the correct moments of the return process. Since they base their market participation on the price trend of an asset, chartists can be regarded as adaptive investors. Formally, we assume that both investors $i \in \{1, 2\}$ use the simple trading rule to predict the ex-dividend stock price of asset k for period $t + 1$

$$\langle e_k, p_t^i \rangle = \sum_{s=1}^{\tau} \mathcal{D}_{ks}^i \langle e_k, p_{t-s} \rangle, \tag{3.19}$$

where $\mathcal{D}_{ks}^i \in \mathbb{R}_+$ is referred to investor i's subjective weight of the k-th asset at time $t-s$. Therefore, the matrix $\mathcal{D}^i = (\mathcal{D}_{ks}^i)_{\substack{k=1,\dots n, \\ s=1,\dots,\tau}} \in \mathbb{R}_+^{n \times \tau}$ denotes investor i's *weight matrix*. The predicted cum-dividend stock price of asset k then becomes

$$\langle e_k, \bar{q}_t^i \rangle = \Psi_1^i \left(\{p_s, d_s, \bar{q}_s^i, V_s^i\}_{t-\tau}^{t-1} \right) := \sum_{s=1}^{\tau} \mathcal{D}_{ks}^i \langle e_k, p_{t-s} \rangle + \langle e_k, d_t \rangle. \tag{3.20}$$

Moreover, we assume that the dividend process is predictable, i.e. d_{t+1} is known in period t, such that

$$\mathbb{E}_t[d_{t+1}] = d_{t+1} \quad \text{for all} \quad t \geq 0,$$

and thus, $\mathbb{V}\mathrm{ar}_t[d_{t+1}] = 0$ for all $t \geq 0$. Therefore, the uncertainty of the economy rests solely with the noise traders' transactions described by a stochastic process $\{\xi_t\}_{t \geq 0}$ with mean $\mathbb{E}_{t-1}[\xi_t] = \bar{\xi}$ and a non-degenerate covariance matrix $\mathbb{V}\mathrm{ar}_{t-1}[\xi_t] = \Lambda$. We restrict our attention to the case in which second moment beliefs are constant over time, i.e. $V_t^i \equiv V^i$ for $i = 1, 2$ and all $t \geq 0$. The forecasting behaviour of investors hence reduces to updating first moment beliefs as given in (3.20). This yields the following system

$$\begin{cases} p_{c,t} & = G_c\left(\xi_t, (\bar{q}_t^i, V_t^i)_{i=1}^2\right) \\ x_{c,t}^i & = \phi_c^i\left(p_{c,t}; \bar{q}_t^i, V_t^i\right) \\ \langle e_k, \bar{q}_t^i \rangle & = \sum_{s=1}^{\mathcal{T}} \mathcal{D}_{ks}^i \langle e_k, p_{t-s} \rangle + \langle e_k, d_t \rangle \\ V_t^i & = V^i = \text{constant}, \end{cases} \tag{3.21}$$

of stochastic difference equations for $k = 1, \ldots, n$ and $i = 1, 2$. Equations (3.21) describe the evolution of prices and allocations in the stock market and define a *time-one map of a dynamical system* in a random environment. Recall that the price p_t was not observed when the forecast in period t was made. Moreover, the forecasting weights are given by

Description	Value	Parameter
Safe rate	1.003	R_f
Market portfolio	$(2, 2)^\top$	x_{m}
Risk tolerance	$(1, 1)^\top$	$a = (a^1, a^2)^\top$
Initial prices	$(0.5, 0.5)^\top$	p_0
Short-sale limit	-0.25	χ

Table 3.1: Fixed parameter values

$$\mathcal{D}^1 = \begin{pmatrix} 0.3 & 0.3 & 0.2 & 0.1 & 0.1 \\ 0.3 & 0.3 & 0.2 & 0.1 & 0.1 \end{pmatrix}$$

and

$$\mathcal{D}^2 = \begin{pmatrix} 0.1 & 0.1 & 0.2 & 0.3 & 0.3 \\ 0.1 & 0.1 & 0.2 & 0.3 & 0.3 \end{pmatrix}.$$

To gain insight into the long-run consequences of short-sale constraints, we present a numerical case study. For simplicity we consider a financial market with two risky assets in which asset 2 is regulated. The analysis can then be easily extended to the case of an arbitrary but finite number of assets. The numerical experiments of this section are carried out by the R-based software package *Simtools* (SCHILLING AND WENZELBURGER (2018)). We analyse three different parameter sets, which merely differ in the subjective second moment beliefs. Table 3.1 lists the parameters that are assumed to be constant for all numerical experiments. These parameters indicate that both investors have identical risk tolerances $a^1 = a^2 = 1$ and determine their forecast at time t based on the $\tau = 5$ previous price-observations. The choice of the weight matrices $\mathcal{D}^i$, $i = 1, 2$, implies that investors have different expectations formation. Investor 2 gives more weight to the time periods closer to the date of price formation, while investor one determines her expectations in the reverse way. Moreover, we suppose that the dividend payments are modelled by a bivariate normal distribution which is restricted to positive real numbers. Mean and standard deviations of the dividend processes are given by $\mu_d^{(1)} = 1 = \mu_d^{(2)}$ and $\sigma_d^{(1)} = 2 = \sigma_d^{(2)}$, respectively. This assumption as well as the parameter choice in Table 3.1 is dictated by the stability properties of the model.

Case 1: Homogeneous expectations

As a benchmark we investigate the case in which investors agree on the same covariance matrix

$$V^1 = V^2 = \frac{1}{4}\begin{pmatrix} 4 & 1 \\ 1 & 2 \end{pmatrix}.$$

Initially, in accordance with other models in financial literature (e.g. ANUFRIEV AND TUINSTRA (2013)), we do not account for noise traders' transactions. Figure 3.2 portrays the dynamics of asset price deviations as well as the evolution of investors' shares of the *regulated security*.

In the static case, homogeneous expectations lead to an overpriced regulated security while unregulated asset prices remain unchanged (see Proposition 4). The same effect can be observed in a dynamic framework: Figure 3.2(a) shows that the expression $p_{c,t}^{(1)} - p_t^{(1)}$ has a magnitude of 10^{-15} and hence is approximately zero. Thus, the overpricing of the unregulated asset is negligible. On the other hand, the regulated asset price is distorted upwards whenever the short-sale constraint becomes binding (Figures 3.2(b) and (c)).

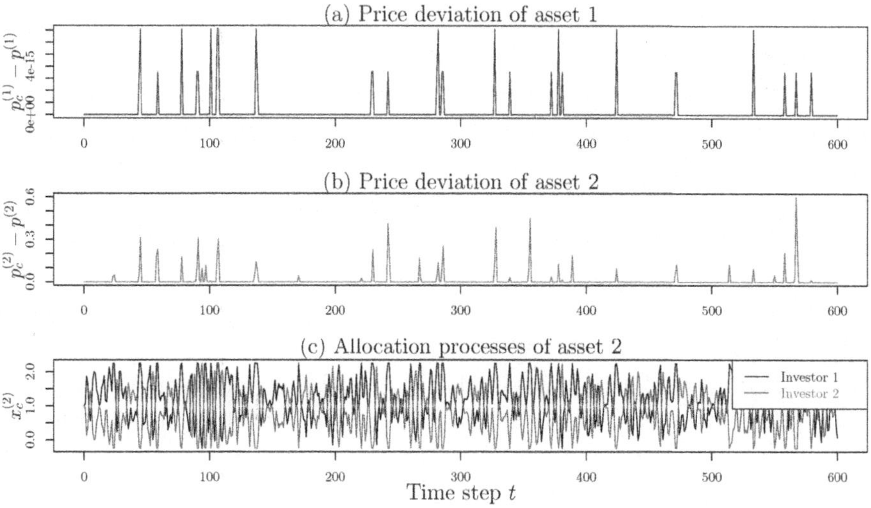

Figure 3.2: Case 1 in the absence of noise traders

The above results, however, cannot be reproduced if noise traders participate in the financial market. Suppose noise traders' transactions are bivariate discrete uniformly distributed with values[5]

$$\{-0.25, -0.1, 0, 0.1, 0.25\}. \tag{3.22}$$

Then Figure 3.3 shows that the constraint on short-sales may distort the asset prices both upwards and downwards, whenever noise traders participate in the financial market.

Case 2: Contrary asset correlations

We proceed with the case in which investors have adverse estimates about the correlation of risky assets and no noise traders participate in the financial market. As a specific example we set

$$V^1 = \frac{1}{10}\begin{pmatrix} 4 & 1 \\ 1 & 2 \end{pmatrix} \quad \text{and} \quad V^2 = \frac{1}{10}\begin{pmatrix} 4 & -1 \\ -1 & 2 \end{pmatrix}. \tag{3.23}$$

In the static model with short-sale constraints, Example 7 showed that the price of the *regulated asset* is distorted upwards whenever investors disagree

[5] Note that this choice does not limit our model, as the obtained results carry over to other choices of discrete distributions. However, we restrict our attention to noise traders' transactions which satisfy the short-sale constraint.

upon the sign of the asset correlation. As illustrated in Figure 3.4(b), we observe overpricing of the *regulated asset* in the dynamic framework as well.

For the *unregulated asset* it was shown in Example 7 that it becomes more expensive if and only if the long-seller expects a positive and the short-seller a negative correlation between the risky assets. Note that, in a dynamic framework, the short-seller may switch over time. Therefore, as depicted in Figure 3.4(a), the short-sale constraint will distort the price of the *unregulated security* upwards as well as downwards. The expectations formation of the first moment thus have an indirect effect on over- or underpricing of asset prices. This noticeable feature is neglected in a static framework. While in a one-period model, the short-seller is identified once and overpricing depends solely on the covariance matrix of the investors, in a dynamic framework the short-seller may switch over time, leading to over- or underpricing even though the covariance matrices remain constant.
Allowing noise traders to participate in the financial market leads, as in the case of homogeneous expectations, to mixed effects on asset prices. Therefore, we omit the related graphical representation.

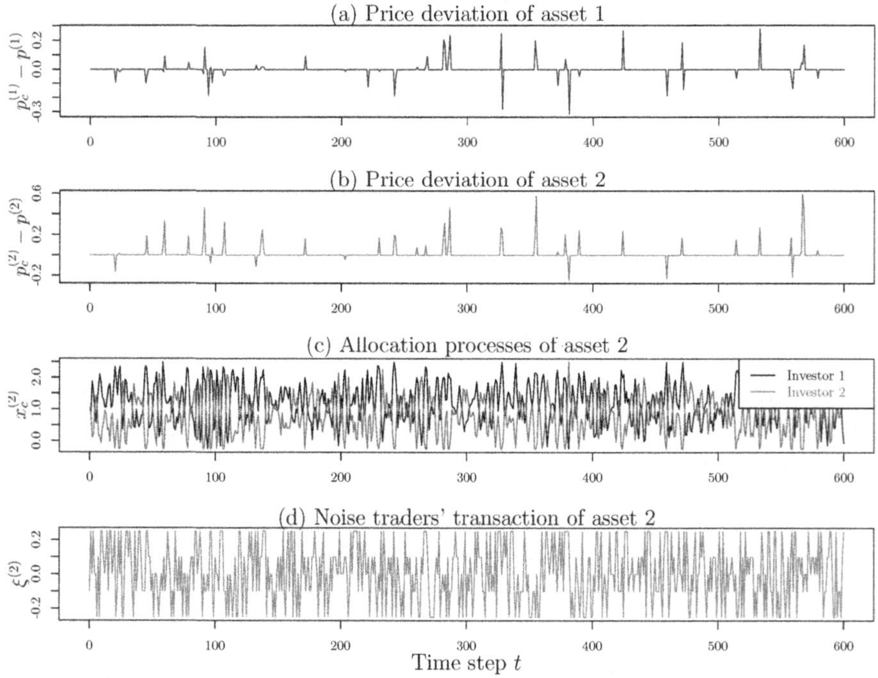

Figure 3.3: Case 1 in the presence of noise traders

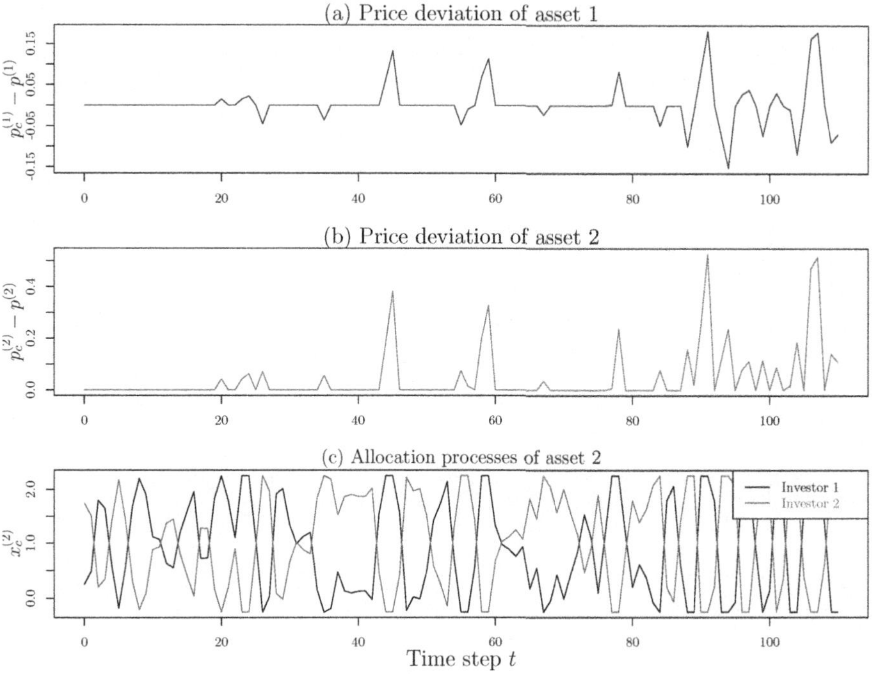

Figure 3.4: Case 2 in the absence of noise traders

Case 3: Strong disagreement on asset volatilities

So far, the numerical results suggest that imposing a short-sale constraint can distort the equilibrium price of the *regulated* asset downwards only if noise traders interact in the financial market. To clarify that restricted short-selling may also distort asset prices downwards in the absence of noise traders participation, we examine the following scenario of heterogeneous covariance matrices

$$V^1 = \begin{pmatrix} 4 & 1 \\ 1 & \frac{3}{10} \end{pmatrix} \quad \text{and} \quad V^2 = \begin{pmatrix} \frac{3}{10} & 1 \\ 1 & 4 \end{pmatrix}. \tag{3.24}$$

We see that there is a strong disagreement about the risk properties of securities among investors. Analysing the dynamics of asset prices and allocations for the covariance matrices given in (3.24), we observe in Figure 3.5 that restricting short-sales may reduce asset prices of both risky securities. This numerical result points out that the short-sale constraint as an instrument to prevent a decline of asset prices will not only miss its target but may even amplify underpricing.

It is worth-noting that in case 3 the downward price-distortion is unaffected by the entrance of noise traders into the market. This can be ex-

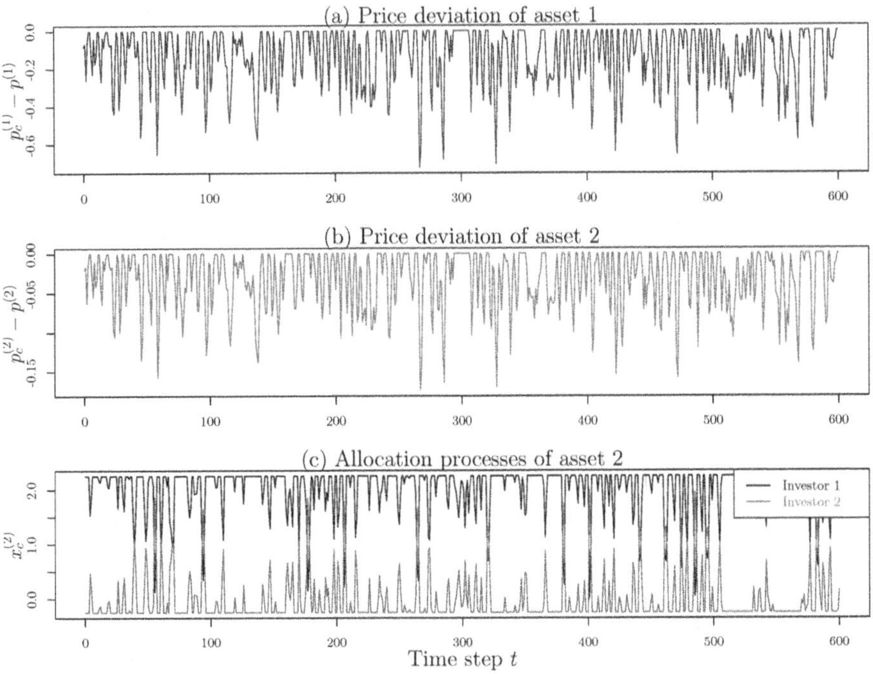

Figure 3.5: Case 3 in the absence of noise traders

plained as follows: the strong disagreement on asset volatilities leads to a wide dispersion of respective asset shares (sample means of $\hat{\mu}^2_{600} \approx 0.1$ and $\hat{\mu}^1_{600} \approx 1.9$, see Figure 3.5(c)). Therefore, fluctuations in asset holdings of noise traders do not lead to alternating short-sellers.

3.3 Price volatility

In addition to the concerns that short-selling can contribute to a further decline of asset prices, regulators generally claim that limited short-selling decreases price volatility. For this reason, in view of the market turbulence in June 2010, the *Bundesanstalt für Finanzdienstleistungsaufsicht (BaFin)* in Germany announced a prohibition of short-selling for 11 German financial stocks, stating that:

> "In the current situation of the capital markets, an influence exercised on the prices of the securities by short-selling leads to excessive price movements that could jeopardise the stability of the financial system. BAFIN (2010)."

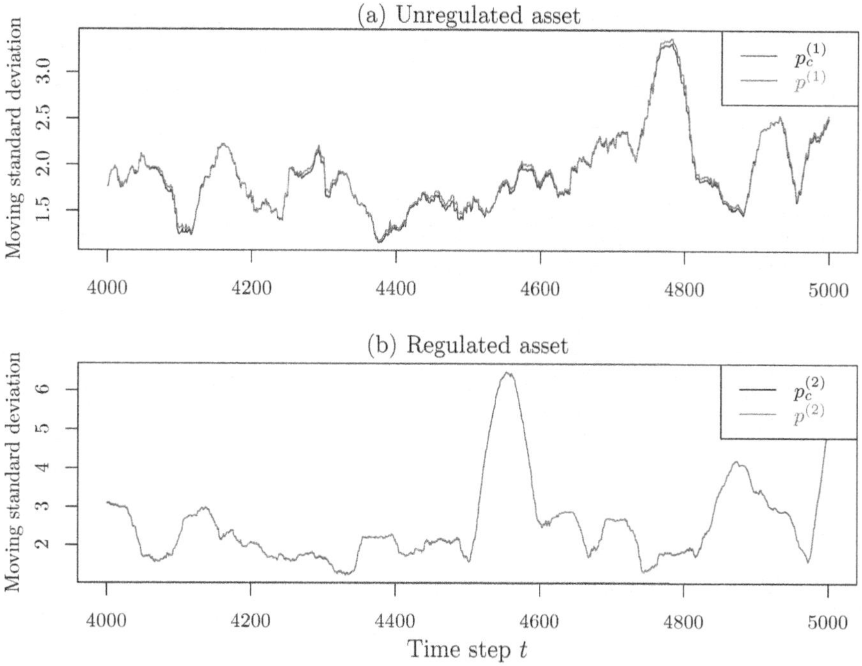

Figure 3.6: Asset price volatility in the long-run

In this context, we aim at examining the influence of the short-sale constraint on the price volatility. While a large number of publications focuses on Miller's overpricing theory, only a small amount of scientific work studies the relationship between limited short-selling and price stability, the latter concluding that restricted short-selling may have mixed effect on price fluctuations. CHANG ET AL. (2006) for example, show that under the assumption of symmetric information of investors, short-sale constraints lead to a decrease in the stock price volatility. On the other hand, the authors suggest that in markets with higher information asymmetry regulating short-sales can in fact decrease stability. In a comprehensive empirical study, SAFFI AND SIGURDSSON (2010) show that imposing short-sale constraints is not associated with a decrease in price stability. Yet, most of these models found in the literature are either static in nature (e.g. KRAUS AND RUBIN (2003) and CHANG ET AL. (2006)) or provide merely empirical evidence (e.g. among others HO (1996), CHAROENROOK AND DAOUK (2009) and GULEN AND MAYHEW (2000)). A first step towards dynamical analysis was taken by ANUFRIEV AND TUINSTRA (2013), whose model, however, is limited to the one-asset case.

In our dynamical setting we consider a financial market with two risky assets in which two investors with adaptive expectations interact. The price process volatility is captured by the moving standard deviation with a window of length 50. It is derived by calculating a 50 time period standard deviation of the data item. On the basis of this volatility measure we calculate the price fluctuations both with and without short-sale constraints, considering the parameters of Table 3.1 as well as the second moments (3.23).

A long-run simulation with 5000 iterations shows that the moving standard deviation of the regulated asset remains unaffected, whereas the volatility of the unregulated security slightly decreases (see Figure 3.6(a)). Similar results were obtained for different parameter sets throughout various simulations, verifying the robustness of the observed phenomenon. Yet another observation was that a change in the length of the window in the moving standard deviation does not influence the qualitative results.

4 Security Market Line

The empirical validity of the Capital Asset Pricing Model (CAPM) is one of the most widely discussed topics in the financial literature. The empirical studies treating CAPM and its extensions are widespread. Based on regression analysis, these tests examine whether there is a linear relationship between risk and mean return. However, the validity of the associated empirical studies is questionable for several reasons. ROLL (1977) and ROSS (1977), among others, arrived at the conclusion that the market portfolio is unobservable. Since in practice, the market portfolio would contain all available assets, it is replaced by a suitable proxy (e.g. the S&P 500 or DAX). Another reason why empirical studies fail is that testing the validity of the CAPM is equivalent to testing whether the market portfolio is mean-variance efficient, which in general, is not fulfilled. This is better known as ROLL'S CRITIQUE.

To approach this problem, WENZELBURGER (2018B) introduced a *modified market portfolio*, which unlike the standard market portfolio of the CAPM, accounts for diverse and erroneous beliefs of investors and is mean-variance efficient in the sense of MARKOWITZ (1952). In this way, a time-dependent security market line was established that allows for a decomposition into *systematic* and *non-systematic* risk. Apart from a non-degenerate covariance structure and the possibility of unrestricted short-selling, it requires no assumptions on how financial markets set prices. However, if short-sales are constrained, the modified market portfolio may become inefficient. In the present chapter, we therefore aim at the derivation of a time-dependent security market line on the regulated financial market. For this purpose we replace the modified market portfolio by a constrained-efficient portfolio. This derivation is missing so far in the literature. By supposing homogeneous expectations among all investors, SCHNABEL (1984) pursued this question. However, as seen in Chapter 2, this assumption prevents the short-sale restrictions to be binding. Also FAMA AND FRENCH (2004) emphasised that the finance

G. Hunanyan, *The Consequences of Short-Sale Constraints on the Stability of Financial Markets*, Finanzwirtschaft, Banken und Bankmanagement | Finance, Banks and Bank Management, https://doi.org/10.1007/978-3-658-27956-1_5

theory does not provide an answer regarding the existence of a security market line on a financial market in the presence of short-sale constraints.[1]
The structure of the chapter is as follows: Section 4.1 analyses the effects of short-sale constraints on the (individual) systematic risk of variance-minimising as well as Sharpe ratio maximising investors. For a given exogenous stochastic process of asset returns, Section 4.2 re-establishes the time-dependent security market line on a financial market with *restricted* short-selling whereas Section 4.3 re-establishes it on a financial market with *prohibited* short-selling.

4.1 Systematic risk

Diversification is a risk management technique accomplished by mixing a variety of financial instruments within a single portfolio. It aims at the reduction of portfolio risk by taking short and long positions in multiple risky assets. Limiting short-sales might therefore reduce diversification possibilities and increase the *non-diversifiable* (or *systematic*) risk. In this section we provide a theoretical foundation which allows us to analyse the consequences of short-sale constraints on the systematic risk of *risk-minimising* and *Sharpe ratio maximising* investors.

As before, we consider an economy with $n+1$ retradeable assets indexed by $k = 0, 1, \ldots, n$. Time is divided into discrete periods $t = 0, 1, 2, \ldots$. In Chapter 3 the evolution of asset prices was modelled as an outcome of heterogeneous interacting agents. Instead of a price process generated by trading activities of agents, we consider asset returns which are stipulated by an exogenous stochastic process[2]

$$\left\{\left(r_t^{(1)}, \ldots, r_t^{(n)}\right)\right\}_{t\geq 0}, \tag{4.1}$$

where $r_t^{(k)}, k \in \{1, \ldots, n\}$ denotes the return on the k-th asset realised in period t. The covariance between the return on the k-th and l-th asset condi-

[1] "But when there is no short-selling of risky assets and no risk-free asset, the algebra of portfolio efficiency says that portfolios made up of efficient portfolios are not typically efficient. This means that the market portfolio, which is a portfolio of the efficient portfolios chosen by investors, is not typically efficient. And the CAPM relation between expected return and market beta is lost. This does not rule out predictions about expected return and betas with respect to other efficient portfolios - if theory can specify portfolios that must be efficient if the market is to clear. But so far this has proven impossible." Fama and French (2004)

[2] For a relation to agent-based finance see Wenzelburger (2018b).

tional on information available at time t is denoted by $\Sigma_{kl,t} = \mathbb{C}\mathrm{ov}_t[r_{t+1}^{(k)}, r_{t+1}^{(l)}]$ so that

$$\Sigma_t := (\Sigma_{kl,t})_{k,l=1,\dots,n} \tag{4.2}$$

is the *conditional covariance matrix of returns*, at date t. Let $\omega \in \mathbb{R}^n$ denote a vector of portfolio weights of risky assets, where $\omega^{(k)}$ denotes the *relative amount* of funds invested into the k-th risky security. Then $\omega^{(0)} = 1 - \sum_{k=1}^{n} \omega^{(k)}$ corresponds to the relative amount invested into the risk-free bond $k = 0$. With r_f being the return on the bond, the return on portfolio ω realised in period $t+1$ can be computed by

$$R_{t+1}(\omega) = \omega^{(0)} r_f + \sum_{k=1}^{n} \omega^{(k)} r_{t+1}^{(k)} = r_f + \sum_{k=1}^{n} \omega^{(k)} (r_{t+1}^{(k)} - r_f). \tag{4.3}$$

Assuming that short-selling of the risk-free bond is allowed, the vector of expected excess returns conditional on information available at time t is defined by

$$\Pi_t := \left(\left(\mathbb{E}_t[r_{t+1}^{(1)}] - r_f \right), \dots, \left(\mathbb{E}_t[r_{t+1}^{(n)}] - r_f \right) \right).$$

The conditional expected return on $\omega \in \mathbb{R}^n$ is then given by

$$\begin{aligned} \mathbb{E}_t[R_{t+1}(\omega)] &= r_f + \sum_{k=1}^{n} (\mathbb{E}_t[r_{t+1}^{(k)}] - r_f)\omega^{(k)} \\ &= r_f + \langle \Pi_t, \omega \rangle, \end{aligned}$$

and its conditional variance takes the form

$$\mathbb{V}\mathrm{ar}_t[R_{t+1}(\omega)] = \langle \omega, \Sigma_t \omega \rangle.$$

For simplicity, we assume that there are no redundant assets, that is, no asset return can be obtained as a linear combination of returns on other assets. This assumption is equivalent to require a non-degenerate covariance structure.

Assumption 6. *The return process $\{r_t\}_{t \geq 0}$ of n risky assets is such that each conditional covariance matrix Σ_t, is positive definite in any period $t \geq 0$.*

Assuming that short-selling of risky assets is permitted and the return process satisfies the hypothesis of Assumption 6, Wenzelburger (2018b) introduced the *reference portfolio*

$$\omega_t^{\mathrm{ref}} := \begin{cases} \frac{1}{\sqrt{\langle \Pi_t, \Sigma_t^{-1} \Pi_t \rangle}} \Sigma_t^{-1} \Pi_t & \text{if } \Pi_t \neq 0, \\ 0 & \text{otherwise.} \end{cases} \tag{4.4}$$

Let $R_{t+1}^{\mathrm{ref}} := R_{t+1}(\omega_t^{\mathrm{ref}})$ denote the return on ω_t^{ref} realised in period $t+1$. Then the conditional expected return and the conditional standard deviation of the reference portfolio are given by

$$\mathbb{E}_t[R_{t+1}^{\mathrm{ref}}] = r_f + \langle \Pi_t, \omega_t^{\mathrm{ref}} \rangle = r_f + \sqrt{\langle \Pi_t, \Sigma_t^{-1} \Pi_t \rangle} \tag{4.5}$$

and

$$\sqrt{\mathbb{V}\mathrm{ar}_t[R_{t+1}^{\mathrm{ref}}]} = \sqrt{\langle \omega_t^{\mathrm{ref}}, \Sigma_t \omega_t^{\mathrm{ref}} \rangle} = 1, \tag{4.6}$$

respectively. In the absence of short-sale constraints it was shown that ω_t^{ref} is mean-variance efficient for the consecutive periods t and $t+1$. Therefore, its risk-return profile $(1, \mathbb{E}_t[R_{t+1}^{\mathrm{ref}}])$ lies on the straight line

$$\mu = r_f + \rho_t \sigma, \tag{4.7}$$

where $\rho_t := \sqrt{\langle \Pi_t, \Sigma_t^{-1} \Pi_t \rangle}$ denotes the conditional price of risk. The straight line (4.7) relates the conditional standard deviation of a mean-variance efficient portfolio to its average return and is therefore referred to as the *capital allocation line* of period t. The standard deviation as a measure of risk, however, does not provide any information about the systematic risk of a portfolio.

The following proposition is taken from WENZELBURGER (2018B) and shows that replacing the classical market portfolio by the reference portfolio ω_t^{ref} allows for a time-dependent dynamic decomposition into systematic and non-systematic risk.

Proposition 6 (WENZELBURGER (2018B)). *Let the hypothesis of Assumption 6 be satisfied. Then for each $t \geq 0$ and $k = 1, \ldots, n$,*

$$\mathbb{E}_t[r_{t+1}^{(k)}] - r_f = \beta_t^{(k)} (\mathbb{E}_t[R_{t+1}^{\mathrm{ref}}] - r_f). \tag{4.8}$$

If $\Pi_t \neq 0$ the beta-coefficient is given by

$$\beta_t^{(k)} := \frac{\mathbb{C}\mathrm{ov}_t[r_{t+1}^{(k)}, R_{t+1}^{\mathrm{ref}}]}{\mathbb{V}\mathrm{ar}_t[R_{t+1}^{\mathrm{ref}}]} = \mathbb{C}\mathrm{ov}_t[r_{t+1}^{(k)}, R_{t+1}^{\mathrm{ref}}]. \tag{4.9}$$

If $\Pi_t = 0$, then $\beta_t^{(k)} = 0$ for all assets k.

The coefficient $\beta_t^{(k)}$ is referred to as *conditional beta coefficient of security k*. Proposition 6 states that the beta coefficient of any asset must lie on the security market line (4.8) and thus, from an empirical point of view, can be seen as the regression coefficient of $r_{t+1}^{(k)}$ on R_{t+1}^{ref}. The linearity of expected excess return on asset k to its beta coefficient $\beta_t^{(k)}$ follows directly from the efficiency of ω_t^{ref}. Therefore, apart from a non-degenerate covariance structure, no assumption on how financial markets determine prices is required.

The beta coefficients have some desirable properties. On the one hand, the ordering "security k is riskier than security l" is complete if and only if $\beta_t^{(k)}$ and $\beta_t^{(l)}$ are associated with the same reference portfolio ω_t^{ref}. On the other hand, Equation (4.3) suggests that the beta coefficient of a portfolio is equal to the weighted average of the betas of the individual assets that make up the portfolio. Consequently, the security market line holds for portfolio returns as well.

Theorem 9 (WENZELBURGER (2018B)). *Let the hypothesis of Assumption 6 be satisfied. Then for each $t \geq 0$, the excess return on any portfolio ω satisfies*

$$\mathbb{E}_t[R_{t+1}(\omega)] - r_f = \beta_t(\mathbb{E}_t[R_{t+1}^{\mathrm{ref}}] - r_f), \tag{4.10}$$

where

$$\beta_t := \frac{\mathbb{C}\mathrm{ov}_t[R_{t+1}(\omega), R_{t+1}^{\mathrm{ref}}]}{\mathbb{V}\mathrm{ar}_t[R_{t+1}^{\mathrm{ref}}]} = \mathbb{C}\mathrm{ov}_t[R_{t+1}(\omega), R_{t+1}^{\mathrm{ref}}] \tag{4.11}$$

if $\Pi_t \neq 0$ and $\beta_t = 0$ whenever $\Pi_t = 0$.

It is worth-noting that since $\mathbb{E}_t[R_{t+1}^{\mathrm{ref}}] = r_f + \rho_t$, the expected return on *any* portfolio satisfies

$$\mathbb{E}_t[R_{t+1}(\omega)] = r_f + \rho_t \beta_t.$$

Therefore, ρ_t can also be interpreted as the *price of systematic risk* whenever the portfolio's β_t is related to ω_t^{ref}. While the capital allocation line (4.7) displays the risk-return profiles of *efficient portfolios*, the security market line (4.10) relates the risk premium of *any* portfolio to the risk premium of the reference portfolio. The proportionality factor β_t can then be used as a measure of non-diversifiable risk in the following sense:

Given a stochastic return process $\{r_t\}_{t\geq 0}$, one may choose a series of random variables $\{\varepsilon_t\}_{t\geq 0}$ such that

$$R_{t+1}(\omega) = r_f + \beta_t(R_{t+1}^{\mathrm{ref}} - r_f) + \varepsilon_{t+1}, \tag{4.12}$$

for all $t \geq 0$. The security market line (4.10) implies that $\mathbb{C}\mathrm{ov}_t[\varepsilon_{t+1}, R_{t+1}^{\mathrm{ref}}] = 0$ and

$$\mathbb{E}_t[\varepsilon_{t+1}] = 0.$$ [3]

[3] The variable ε_t can be seen as a regression residual when regressing the portfolio return $R_{t+1}(\omega)$ on the reference return R_{t+1}^{ref}. The residual is uncorrelated to the reference return R_{t+1}^{ref} and does, on average, not affect the mean return of a portfolio in a linear cross-sectional regression model.

Therefore, taking the conditional variance on both sides of (4.12) yields

$$\begin{aligned}\mathbb{V}\mathrm{ar}_t[R_{t+1}(\omega)] &= (\beta_t)^2\mathbb{V}\mathrm{ar}_t[R^{\mathrm{ref}}_{t+1}] + \mathbb{V}\mathrm{ar}_t[\varepsilon_{t+1}] + \mathbb{C}\mathrm{ov}_t[\varepsilon_{t+1}, R^{\mathrm{ref}}_{t+1}] \\ &= (\beta_t)^2\mathbb{V}\mathrm{ar}_t[R^{\mathrm{ref}}_{t+1}] + \mathbb{V}\mathrm{ar}_t[\varepsilon_{t+1}].\end{aligned} \tag{4.13}$$

The first term, $(\beta_t)^2\mathbb{V}\mathrm{ar}_t[R^{\mathrm{ref}}_{t+1}]$, is referred to as *non-diversifiable* risk in period t. Using (4.11) it can be written as

$$(\beta_t)^2\mathbb{V}\mathrm{ar}_t[R^{\mathrm{ref}}_{t+1}] = \mathbb{C}\mathrm{or}_t[R_{t+1}(\omega), R^{\mathrm{ref}}_{t+1}]^2\mathbb{V}\mathrm{ar}_t[R_{t+1}(\omega)]. \tag{4.14}$$

This risk cannot be eliminated through diversification and is therefore associated with the entire market. The second part, $\mathbb{V}\mathrm{ar}_t[\varepsilon_{t+1}]$, is termed the *diversifiable* risk in period t and, by use of Equation (4.14), can be formulated as

$$\mathbb{V}\mathrm{ar}_t[\varepsilon_{t+1}] = (1 - \mathbb{C}\mathrm{or}_t[R_{t+1}(\omega), R^{\mathrm{ref}}_{t+1}]^2)\mathbb{V}\mathrm{ar}_t[R_{t+1}(\omega)]. \tag{4.15}$$

This risk is that amount of volatility that can be reduced through diversification: if the portfolio ω is *perfectly diversified*, that is $\mathbb{C}\mathrm{or}_t[R_{t+1}(\omega), R^{\mathrm{ref}}_{t+1}] = 1$, Equation (4.15) implies $\mathbb{V}\mathrm{ar}_t[\varepsilon_{t+1}] = 0$.

The following proposition shows that efficient portfolios solely contain non-diversifiable risk.

Proposition 7. *Let the hypothesis of Assumption 6 be satisfied. Then any mean-variance efficient portfolio ω_t^* solely contains non-diversifiable risk with respect to ω_t^{ref}. In particular, the non-diversifiable risk is given by*

$$\mathbb{V}\mathrm{ar}_t[R_{t+1}(\omega_t^*)] = (\beta_t)^2 = \mathbb{C}\mathrm{ov}_t[R_{t+1}(\omega_t^*), R^{\mathrm{ref}}_{t+1}]^2. \tag{4.16}$$

Proof. Let ω_t^* be an arbitrary efficient portfolio with conditional expected mean $\mathbb{E}_t[R_{t+1}(\omega_t^*)]$ and conditional standard deviation, $\sqrt{\mathbb{V}\mathrm{ar}_t[R_{t+1}(\omega_t^*)]}$ respectively. The capital allocation line together with the security market line (4.10) implies

$$\mathbb{E}_t[R_{t+1}(\omega_t^*)] - r_f = \rho_t\sqrt{\mathbb{V}\mathrm{ar}_t[R_{t+1}(\omega_t^*)]} = \beta_t(\mathbb{E}_t[R^{\mathrm{ref}}_{t+1}] - r_f), \tag{4.17}$$

for all $t \geq 0$. The efficiency of ω_t^{ref} yields

$$\mathbb{E}_t[R^{\mathrm{ref}}_{t+1}] - r_f = \rho_t\sqrt{\mathbb{V}\mathrm{ar}_t[R^{\mathrm{ref}}_{t+1}]}. \tag{4.18}$$

Inserting (4.18) into Equation (4.17) and rearranging, the variance of ω_t^* becomes

$$\mathbb{V}\mathrm{ar}_t[R_{t+1}(\omega_t^*)] = (\beta_t)^2\mathbb{V}\mathrm{ar}_t[R^{\mathrm{ref}}_{t+1}] = (\beta_t)^2.$$

□

Proposition 7 allows for an alternative interpretation of mean-variance efficient portfolios, as asset allocations without diversifiable risk. However, since every efficient portfolio is collinear to $\Sigma_t^{-1}\Pi_t$ and thus perfectly correlated to ω_t^{ref}, this result is rather intuitive.

The optimal portfolio mix $\Sigma_t^{-1}\Pi_t$ and thus the possibility of unrestricted short-selling is crucial for obtaining perfectly diversified portfolios. Indeed, LEVY (1983) indicates that the determining motive of short-selling is the *diversification motive*, while the traditional *profitability motive* (shorting asset k if $\mathbb{E}_t[r_{t+1}^{(k)}] < r_f$) is secondary. Proponents of a frictionless market claim that the constraint on short-sales will lead to a reduction of diversification possibilities and increase the amount of non-systematic risk. In the remainder of this section we therefore analyse the validity of this hypothesis by considering *risk-minimising* and *Sharpe ratio maximising* investors.

The risk-minimising portfolio which attains the same return as ω_t^{ref} and satisfies the short-sale constraint is given by the solution of the following decision problem

$$\omega_t^{\xi} := \underset{\omega \in \mathbb{R}}{\arg\min}\ \mathbb{V}\text{ar}_t[R_{t+1}(\omega)] \quad \text{s.t.} \quad \mathbb{E}_t[R_{t+1}(\omega)] = \mathbb{E}_t[R_{t+1}^{\text{ref}}], \quad \langle e_n, \omega \rangle \geq \xi. \tag{4.19}$$

The following lemma quantifies the diversifiable risk of ω_t^{ξ} with respect to ω_t^{ref}.

Lemma 5. *Let the hypothesis of Assumption 6 be satisfied and $\mathbb{E}_t[R_{t+1}^{\text{ref}}] > r_f$ be the expected reference return on ω_t^{ref}. Set*

$$\sigma_t^{\xi} = \frac{\xi}{\sqrt{\langle e_n, \Sigma_t^{-1} e_n \rangle}} \quad \text{and} \quad \Omega_t := \left(\begin{array}{c|c} (\Sigma_{t\backslash n})^{-1} & \begin{matrix} 0 \\ \vdots \\ 0 \end{matrix} \\ \hline 0 \cdots 0 & 0 \end{array} \right)$$

where $(\Sigma_{t\backslash n})^{-1} \in \mathbb{R}^{(n-1)\times(n-1)}$ is the covariance matrix on the smaller security market without the n–th risky asset. Then the diversifiable risk of ω_t^{ξ} with respect to ω_t^{ref} is given by

$$\mathbb{V}\text{ar}_t[\varepsilon_{t+1}^{\xi}] = \left(\frac{\sqrt{\langle \Pi_t, \Sigma_t^{-1}\Pi_t \rangle} \langle e_n, \Sigma_t^{-1}\Pi_t \rangle - \xi \langle \Pi_t, \Sigma_t^{-1}\Pi_t \rangle}{\sqrt{\langle \Pi_t, \Omega_t \Pi_t \rangle} \langle e_n, \Sigma_t^{-1}\Pi_t \rangle} \right)^2 + (\sigma_t^{\xi})^2 - 1.$$

In particular, the smaller ξ the larger the residual risk $\mathbb{V}\text{ar}_t[\varepsilon_{t+1}^{\xi}]$. The diversifiable risk for the boundary case $\xi = 0$ is given by

$$\mathbb{V}\text{ar}_t[\varepsilon_{t+1}^{0}] = \frac{\langle \Pi_t, \Sigma_t^{-1}\Pi_t \rangle}{\langle \Pi_t, \Omega_t \Pi_t \rangle} - 1. \tag{4.20}$$

Proof. The computation of the general form of risk-minimising portfolios can be found in Appendix A.1. Setting the prescribed level of expected return to $\mathbb{E}_t[R^{\mathrm{ref}}_{t+1}]$, we obtain ω^{ξ}_t. Since the expected excess return on ω^{ξ}_t equals $\mathbb{E}_t[R^{\mathrm{ref}}_{t+1}] - r_f$, the security market line (4.10) implies that $\beta_t = 1$. The decomposition formula (4.13) therefore, implies

$$\mathbb{V}\mathrm{ar}_t[\varepsilon^{\xi}_{t+1}] = \mathbb{V}\mathrm{ar}_t[R_{t+1}(\omega^{\xi}_t)] - \mathbb{V}\mathrm{ar}_t[R^{\mathrm{ref}}_{t+1}], \tag{4.21}$$

where the conditional variance of ω^{ξ}_t can be computed as

$$\mathbb{V}\mathrm{ar}_t[R_{t+1}(\omega^{\xi}_t)] = \left(\frac{\sqrt{\langle \Pi_t, \Sigma_t^{-1} \Pi_t \rangle} \langle e_n, \Sigma_t^{-1} \Pi_t \rangle - \xi \langle \Pi_t, \Sigma_t^{-1} \Pi_t \rangle}{\sqrt{\langle \Pi_t, \Omega_t \Pi_t \rangle} \langle e_n, \Sigma_t^{-1} \Pi_t \rangle} \right)^2 + (\sigma^{\xi}_t)^2.$$

□

In Appendix A.1 we show that the risk-return profile of portfolio weights ω^{ξ}_t lies on *constrained-capital allocation curve*

$$\mathcal{C}_t(\sigma) = \begin{cases} r_f + \rho_t \sigma & \text{if } \sigma \leq \frac{\xi}{\langle e_n, \Sigma_t^{-1} \Pi_t \rangle}, \\ \mu^{\xi}_t + \underline{\rho}_t \sqrt{\sigma^2 - (\sigma^{\xi}_t)^2} & \text{otherwise}, \end{cases} \tag{4.22}$$

where $\underline{\rho}_t := \sqrt{\langle \Pi_t, \Omega_t \Pi_t \rangle}$ is the conditional price of risk on the smaller financial market and $\mu^{\xi}_t := r_f + \xi \frac{\langle e_n, \Sigma_t^{-1} \Pi_t \rangle}{\langle e_n, \Sigma_t^{-1} e_n \rangle}$.

Finance literature identifies a *risk-minimising* investor as the one who seeks for an optimal portfolio mix in order to diversify and reduce the total risk of a portfolio. On the other hand, the primary motive of a Sharpe ratio maximiser to short an asset is the *profitability motive*: since any mean-variance efficient portfolio attains the highest possible Sharpe ratio[4], traders short-sale an asset to gain a larger profit. Under a theoretical setting the Sharpe ratio is emphasised as "the optimal portfolio performance measure". (LEVY (2017), p 14). We will therefore analyse the impact of short-sale constraints on an investor who maximises the Sharpe ratio of a portfolio.

Formally, the Sharpe ratio conditional on information at time t associated with the return $R_{t+1}(\omega)$ on portfolio $\omega \in \mathbb{R}$ is defined by

$$\mathrm{SR}(\omega) := \frac{\mathbb{E}_t[R_{t+1}(\omega)] - r_f}{\sqrt{\mathbb{V}\mathrm{ar}_t[R_{t+1}(\omega)]}} = \frac{\langle \Pi_t, \omega \rangle}{\sqrt{\langle \omega, \Sigma_t \omega \rangle}}. \tag{4.23}$$

[4] See e.g. LEVY AND RITOV (2011) or WENZELBURGER (2018B)

In calculating the Sharpe ratio, one can use either the *scaled* or the *unscaled* portfolio weights. The scaled portfolio weights are obtained by multiplying the unscaled portfolio mix with a positive scalar $\lambda \in \mathbb{R}_+$. Therefore, if short-selling of risky assets is unrestricted, any mean-variance efficient portfolio attains the highest possible Sharpe ratio and the investor is indifferent between two efficient portfolios. If, however, short-sales are constrained, a mean-variance efficient portfolio may violate the short-sale constraint and become infeasible for the decision problem

$$\max_{\omega \in \mathbb{R}^n} \mathrm{SR}_t(\omega) \quad \text{s.t.} \quad \omega^{(n)} \geq \xi. \tag{4.24}$$

Proposition 8. *Let $\{r_t\}_{t\geq 0}$ be a return process of n risky assets satisfying the hypothesis of Assumption 6 and suppose that $\langle e_n, \Sigma_t^{-1}\Pi_t \rangle < 0$ at time t.*

1. *If short-selling is restricted such that $\xi < 0$, any portfolio $\omega_t = \underline{\lambda}\Sigma_t^{-1}\Pi_t$ with*
$$0 < \underline{\lambda} \leq \frac{\xi}{\langle e_n, \Sigma_t^{-1}\Pi_t \rangle} \tag{4.25}$$
solves (4.24). In particular, the portfolio weights
$$\theta_t := \frac{\xi}{\langle e_n, \omega_t^{\mathrm{ref}} \rangle} \omega_t^{\mathrm{ref}} \tag{4.26}$$
satisfy the restricted short-selling constraint and attain the highest possible Sharpe ratio $\mathrm{SR}_t(\theta_t) = \rho_t$.

2. *If short-selling is prohibited such that $\xi = 0$, any $\nu_t = \lambda\Omega_t\Pi_t$ with $\lambda > 0$ solves (4.24) and the Sharpe ratio conditional on information at time t satisfies*
$$\mathrm{SR}_t(\lambda\Omega_t\Pi_t) = \underline{\rho}_t < \rho_t \tag{4.27}$$
for all $\lambda > 0$.

In an empirical study, Levy and Ritov (2011) investigate the *costs* of prohibited short-selling. The authors compare the Sharpe ratios of efficient portfolios when short-sales are allowed to those where short-sales are prohibited. Their results suggest that the Sharpe ratio of a portfolio can be more than doubled with unrestricted short-selling. Equation (4.27) provides an analytical explanation for Levy and Ritov's empirical findings. As prohibition on short-sales diminishes the optimal portfolio mix $\Sigma_t^{-1}\Pi_t$, the Sharpe ratio decreases $\underline{\rho}_t < \rho_t$. If, however, short-selling of a reasonable size is allowed, investors are able to hold the optimal portfolio mix leading to the highest possible Sharpe ratio ρ_t.

Note that, in a frictionless market, a Sharpe ratio maximising investor may choose a portfolio with an arbitrary large amount of risk and attain the Sharpe ratio of ρ_t, as long as the portfolio's risk-return profile lies on the capital allocation line $\mu = r_f + \rho_t\sigma$. This phenomenon might also occur if short-sales are prohibited, as the standard deviation $\sqrt{\mathbb{V}\mathrm{ar}_t[R_{t+1}(\nu_t)]} = \lambda\rho_t$ of the portfolio weights $\nu_t = \lambda\Omega_t\Pi_t$ with $\lambda > 0$ is unbounded. Restricted short-selling, however, puts an upper bound on the portfolio risk by scaling down investments into risky assets.

Proposition 9. *Let the hypothesis of Assumption 6 be satisfied and suppose that* $\langle e_n, \Sigma_t^{-1}\Pi_t\rangle < 0$ *in period t. If short-selling is restricted* ($\xi < 0$)*, a Sharpe ratio maximising portfolio* ω *solely contains systematic risk with respect to* ω_t^{ref}*. Moreover, this risk is bounded from above, i.e.*

$$\mathbb{V}\mathrm{ar}_t[R_{t+1}(\omega)] \leq \mathbb{V}\mathrm{ar}_t[R_{t+1}(\theta_t)] = \left(\frac{\xi}{\langle e_n, \omega_t^{\mathrm{ref}}\rangle}\right)^2, \tag{4.28}$$

for all $\omega \in \underset{\omega\in\mathbb{R}^n}{\arg\max} \left\{\mathrm{SR}_t(\omega) \quad \text{s.t.} \quad \omega^{(n)} \geq \xi\right\}$*. If short-selling is prohibited* ($\xi = 0$)*, any Sharpe ratio maximising portfolio* $\nu_t = \lambda\Omega_t\Pi_t$ *has a positive non-systematic risk with respect to* ω_t^{ref}.

Proposition 9 states that restricting short-sales of one asset in a portfolio of multiple securities puts an upper bound on portfolio risk for a Sharpe ratio maximiser. Consequently, as θ_t is mean-variance efficient in the classical sense, a restricted short-sale constraint also limits the systematic risk of Sharpe ratio maximisers. Therefore, while restricted short-selling is beneficial, a full ban on short-sales induces a non-negative systematic risk for Sharpe ratio maximising investors.

So far we examined how the (individual) systematic risk of an investor's portfolio is affected by short-selling limitations. Our results partly confirm short-sellers' hypothesis claiming that short-sale constraints reduce diversification possibilities and increase the systematic risk of investors. Only a restricted short-sale constraint is able to reduce the systematic risk of investors whose motive to short-sale is the profitability motive.

The next two sections focus on the effects of short-sale constraints on the entire market by answering the following question.

1. Do short-sale constraints decrease the systematic risk of the entire financial market?
2. Is it possible to derive a time-dependent security market line on the regulated financial market?

For this purpose, we replace the reference portfolio ω_t^{ref} by a modified reference portfolio which takes the short-sale constraint into account.

4.2 Restricted short-selling

In the previous section we showed that in the presence of restricted short-selling, the portfolio θ_t is constrained-efficient for the consecutive periods t and $t+1$ and that its return has the highest Sharpe ratio ρ_t. Therefore, we consider the vector of portfolio weights

$$\theta_t^{\mathrm{ref}} := \begin{cases} \omega_t^{\mathrm{ref}} & \text{if } \langle e_n, \omega_t^{\mathrm{ref}} \rangle \geq \xi, \\ \frac{\xi}{\langle e_n, \omega_t^{\mathrm{ref}} \rangle} \omega_t^{\mathrm{ref}} & \text{otherwise,} \end{cases} \tag{4.29}$$

referred to as *θ-constrained reference portfolio*. These portfolio weights correspond to the unconstrained modified portfolio whenever ω_t^{ref} satisfies the short-sale constraint and, otherwise, are replaced by the portfolio weights that just meet the short-sale restriction. The amount allocated to or borrowed from the risk-free bond is then given by $\theta_t^{\mathrm{ref}(0)} := 1 - \sum_{k=1}^{n} \langle e_k, \theta_t^{\mathrm{ref}} \rangle$. Note that regardless of a binding short-sale constraint, the θ-constrained reference portfolio has the optimal portfolio mix of risky assets. Therefore, θ^{ref} is mean-variance efficient and its risk-return profile lies on the capital allocation line $\mu = r_f + \rho_t \sigma$. Consequently, Proposition 9 implies that θ_t^{ref} merely contains systematic risk with respect to ω_t^{ref}. This risk corresponds at most the unit risk and is given by

$$\mathbb{V}\mathrm{ar}_t[R_{t+1}(\theta_t^{\mathrm{ref}})] = \begin{cases} 1 & \text{if } \langle e_n, \omega_t^{\mathrm{ref}} \rangle \geq \xi, \\ \left(\frac{\xi}{\langle e_n, \omega_t^{\mathrm{ref}} \rangle} \right)^2 & \text{otherwise.} \end{cases} \tag{4.30}$$

From Equation (4.30) it follows that the systematic risk of θ_t^{ref} is smaller than the systematic risk of ω_t^{ref} whenever short-selling is restricted. This implication is reasonable since then investors scale down the portfolio weights.

The following theorem shows that, due to the smaller systematic risk, the default risk associated with the portfolio θ_t^{ref} is smaller than the default risk associated with ω_t^{ref}. Hence, restricting short-sales puts an upper bound on the default risk.

Theorem 10. *Let the hypothesis of Assumption 6 be satisfied and suppose that $\langle e_n, \Sigma_t^{-1} \Pi_t \rangle < 0$ in period t. Then for any $t \geq 0$ the following holds true*

$$\Pi(\theta_t^{\mathrm{ref}}) \leq \Pi(\omega_t^{\mathrm{ref}}), \tag{4.31}$$

where the inequality is strict whenever $\langle e_n, \omega_t^{\mathrm{ref}} \rangle < \xi$.

The validity of Theorem 10 is independent of the distributional assumption of the return process. This is an essential difference to the results of Section 1.4 where the default risk was analysed under the premise of elliptically distributed returns.

In order to construct a security market line on the regulated financial market we replace the reference portfolio by its θ-constrained counterpart.

Theorem 11. *Let the hypothesis of Assumption 6 be satisfied. Then for each* $t \geq 0$ *and* $k = 1, \ldots, n$,

$$\mathbb{E}_t[r^{(k)}_{t+1}] - r_f = \beta^{(k)}_{\theta,t}(\mathbb{E}_t[R_{t+1}(\theta^{\text{ref}}_t)] - r_f), \tag{4.32}$$

where

$$\beta^{(k)}_{\theta,t} := \frac{\mathbb{C}\text{ov}_t[r^{(k)}_{t+1}, R_{t+1}(\theta^{\text{ref}}_t)]}{\mathbb{V}\text{ar}_t[R_{t+1}(\theta^{\text{ref}}_t)]}. \tag{4.33}$$

Theorem 11 generalises the classical security market line to a time-dependent security market line which accounts for restricted short-selling.[5] The security market line (4.32) relates the expected excess return on any risky asset to the covariance between the return on the corresponding asset and the benchmark portfolio θ^{ref}_t. As in the unrestricted case, this relation is linear and the proportionality factor in period $t \geq 0$ is given by the *conditional θ-constrained beta coefficient $\beta^{(k)}_{\theta,t}$ of asset* $k \in \{1, \ldots, n\}$.

As explained in Section 4.1, the beta coefficient of a portfolio is equal to the weighted average of individual assets' betas that make up the portfolio. Consequently, the security market line is valid for portfolio returns as well.

Corollary 2. *Let the hypothesis of Assumption 6 be satisfied. Then for each* $t \geq 0$, *the excess return on the* portfolio ω *satisfies*

$$\mathbb{E}_t[R_{t+1}(\omega)] - r_f = \beta_{\theta,t}(\mathbb{E}_t[R_{t+1}(\theta^{\text{ref}}_t)] - r_f), \tag{4.34}$$

where

$$\beta_{\theta,t} := \frac{\mathbb{C}\text{ov}_t[R_{t+1}(\omega), R_{t+1}(\theta^{\text{ref}}_t)]}{\mathbb{V}\text{ar}_t[R_{t+1}(\theta^{\text{ref}}_t)]}. \tag{4.35}$$

The coefficient $\beta_{\theta,t}$ is the conditional θ-constrained beta-coefficient of the portfolio ω and allows for a distinction between systematic and non-systematic risk in exactly the same way as in the unrestricted case. More formally, the return on any portfolio ω satisfies

$$\mathbb{V}\text{ar}_t[R_{t+1}(\omega)] = (\beta_{\theta,t})^2 \mathbb{V}\text{ar}_t[R_{t+1}(\theta^{\text{ref}}_t)] + \mathbb{V}\text{ar}_t[\varepsilon_{t+1}], \tag{4.36}$$

[5] Since θ^{ref}_t has the same portfolio mix as ω^{ref}_t, the proof is analogous to the proof in WENZELBURGER (2018B).

where

$$(\beta_{\theta,t})^2 \mathbb{V}\mathrm{ar}_t[R_{t+1}(\theta_t^{\mathrm{ref}})] = \mathbb{C}\mathrm{or}_t[R_{t+1}(\omega), R_{t+1}(\theta_t^{\mathrm{ref}})]^2 \mathbb{V}\mathrm{ar}_t[R_{t+1}(\omega)], \tag{4.37}$$

and

$$\mathbb{V}\mathrm{ar}_t[\varepsilon_{t+1}] = (1 - \mathbb{C}\mathrm{or}_t[R_{t+1}(\omega), R_{t+1}(\theta_t^{\mathrm{ref}})]^2) \mathbb{V}\mathrm{ar}_t[R_{t+1}(\omega)], \tag{4.38}$$

are the systematic and non-systematic risk of ω with respect to θ_t^{ref} at time t.

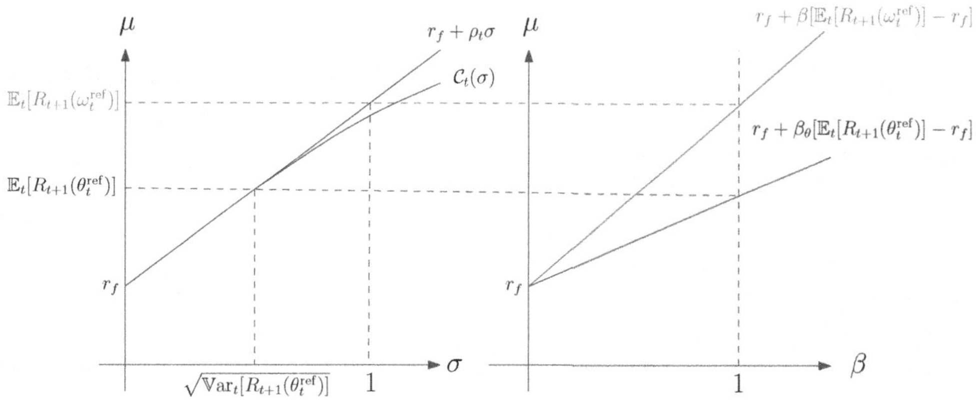

Figure 4.1: Capital allocation and the security market lines

In Figure 4.1 we explain how the capital allocation line can be used to graphically construct the security market line. The capital allocation line relates the expected excess return μ of an efficient portfolio to its standard deviation σ, whereas the security market line relates it to its systematic risk, measured by the portfolio's beta coefficient. While the slope of the capital allocation line is given by the price of risk ρ_t, the slope of the security market line is the risk premium of the θ-constrained reference portfolio. Therefore, at any $t \geq 0$, the beta of the reference portfolio equals one and the security market line is the connecting line between the *risk-free point* $(0, r_f)$ and $(1, \mathbb{E}_t[R_{t+1}(\theta_t^{\mathrm{ref}})])$. The security market line with respect to the unconstrained reference portfolio ω_t^{ref} follows the same construction steps and is displayed in Figure 4.1 for the case that ω_t^{ref} violates the restricted short-sale constraint. Its slope is greater than the slope of the security market line with respect to θ_t^{ref}, indicating that the systematic risk of *any* portfolio ω is smaller relative to θ_t^{ref} than relative to ω_t^{ref}. Note that this does not imply that the portfolio ω becomes less risky, since the total risk of ω remains unchanged.

4.3 Prohibited short-selling

So far we have seen that in the presence of restricted short-selling the modified reference portfolio has the same portfolio decomposition of risky assets as in the unrestricted case. If, however, short-sales are prohibited, constrained efficient portfolios are collinear to the portfolio mix $\Omega_t \Pi_t$; the optimal portfolio decomposition on the smaller financial market. Therefore, the risk-return profile of any constrained-efficient portfolio lies on the straight line

$$\mu = r_f + \underline{\rho}_t \sigma,$$

where, $\underline{\rho}_t = \sqrt{\langle \Pi_t, \Omega_t \Pi_t \rangle}$ denotes the price of risk on the smaller financial market. For a given exogenous stochastic process with no redundant assets, we refer to

$$\nu_t^{\mathrm{ref}} := \begin{cases} \omega_t^{\mathrm{ref}} & \text{if } \langle e_n, \Sigma_t^{-1} \Pi_t \rangle > 0, \\ \frac{1}{\sqrt{\langle \Pi_t, \Omega_t \Pi_t \rangle}} \Omega_t \Pi_t & \text{otherwise,} \end{cases} \tag{4.39}$$

as the *ν-constrained reference portfolio*. These portfolio weights define a constrained-efficient allocation of risky assets in the presence of prohibited short-selling with unit risk. The risk-return profile of ν_t^{ref} is illustrated in Figure 4.2.

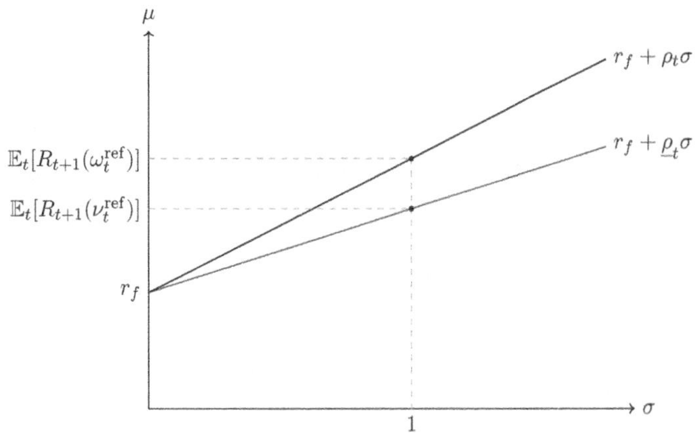

Figure 4.2: Risk-return profile of the ν-constrained reference portfolio

Even though the standard deviations of both portfolio weights ω_t^{ref} and ν_t^{ref}, are normalised to 1, the ν-constrained reference portfolio contains non-systematic risk with respect to ω_t^{ref}.

Proposition 10. *Let the hypothesis of Assumption 6 be satisfied. Then the portfolio weights* ν_t^{ref} *defined in (4.39) cover the non-negative amount of diversifiable risk given by*

$$\mathbb{V}\mathrm{ar}_t[\varepsilon_{t+1}] = 1 - \mathbb{C}\mathrm{or}_t[R_{t+1}(\nu_t^{\mathrm{ref}}), R_{t+1}^{\mathrm{ref}}]^2 \geq 0, \tag{4.40}$$

where the inequality is strict whenever $\langle e_n, \omega_t^{\mathrm{ref}} \rangle < 0$.

The proof of Proposition 10 follows directly from the decomposition formula (4.13). The proposition implies that prohibited short-selling increases the systematic risk of the reference portfolio. Due to the constraint on the regulated financial market, investors are unable to fully diversify. This additional amount of diversifiable risk relative to the unregulated asset market leads to a larger default risk.

Theorem 12. *Consider a return process of* n *risky assets that satisfies the hypothesis of Assumptions 6. Then the coefficient of variation of period-*$t+1$ *wealth that is associated with* ν_t^{ref} *is greater than or equal to the one associated with* ω_t^{ref}*, that is*

$$\frac{\sqrt{\mathbb{V}\mathrm{ar}[R_{t+1}(\nu_t^{\mathrm{ref}})]}}{\mathbb{E}_t[R_{t+1}(\nu_t^{\mathrm{ref}})]} \geq \frac{\sqrt{\mathbb{V}\mathrm{ar}[R_{t+1}^{\mathrm{ref}}]}}{\mathbb{E}_t[R_{t+1}^{\mathrm{ref}}]}. \tag{4.41}$$

In particular, if the return process is multivariate elliptically distributed, the default risk associated with ν_t^{ref} *is greater than or equal to the default risk associated with* ω_t^{ref}*, that is*

$$\Pi(\nu_t^{\mathrm{ref}}) \geq \Pi(\omega_t^{\mathrm{ref}}). \tag{4.42}$$

The above inequalities are strict whenever $\langle e_n, \omega_t^{\mathrm{ref}} \rangle < 0$.

Proposition 10 and Theorem 12 show that a prohibition on short-selling adversely affects the financial market by reducing diversification possibilities. While restrictions on short-sales reduce the systematic risk as well as the default risk, a full ban on short-sales increases both, leading to a more volatile financial market.

In the remaining of this section we will show that a time-dependent security market line can also be derived on the asset market with a full ban on shorting the n-th risky asset. We start with the security market for individual assets and prove first that an explicit linear relationship between an asset's expected excess return and its beta is obtained solely for the unregulated securities $k = 1, \ldots, n-1$.

Theorem 13. *Consider a return process of n risky assets that satisfies the hypothesis of Assumption 6. Then for each $t \geq 0$,*

$$\mathbb{E}_t[r_{t+1}^{(k)}] - r_f = \beta_{\nu,t}^{(k)} \left(\mathbb{E}_t[R_{t+1}(\nu_t^{\text{ref}})] - r_f\right), \tag{4.43}$$

for all $k = 1, \ldots, n-1$ and

$$\mathbb{E}_t[r_{t+1}^{(n)}] - r_f = \beta_{\nu,t}^{(n)} \left(\mathbb{E}_t[R_{t+1}(\nu_t^{\text{ref}})] - r_f\right) + \frac{\langle e_n, \Sigma_t^{-1}\Pi_t\rangle}{\langle e_n, \Sigma_t^{-1} e_n\rangle}, \tag{4.44}$$

for the regulated asset n, where

$$\beta_{\nu,t}^{(k)} := \frac{\mathbb{C}\text{ov}_t[r_{t+1}^{(k)}, R_{t+1}(\nu_t^{\text{ref}})]}{\mathbb{V}\text{ar}_t[R_{t+1}(\nu_t^{\text{ref}})]}. \tag{4.45}$$

The coefficient $\beta_{\nu,t}^{(k)}$ at time t is referred to as the *ν-constrained beta coefficient of the k-th asset*. The linear relationship (4.43) for unregulated assets follows directly from the efficiency of ν_t^{ref} on the frictionless market with $n-1$ assets. The security market line (4.44) for the regulated asset is, however, defined implicitly, since $\mathbb{E}_t[r_{t+1}^{(n)}] - r_f = \Pi_t^{(n)}$ is included in the term $\langle e_n, \Sigma_t^{-1}\Pi_t\rangle$. If the stochastic return process is such that all assets are uncorrelated, the conditional covariance matrix is diagonal and therefore

$$\frac{\langle e_n, \Sigma_t^{-1}\Pi_t\rangle}{\langle e_n, \Sigma_t^{-1} e_n\rangle} = \langle e_n, \Pi_t\rangle = \mathbb{E}_t[r_{t+1}^{(n)}] - r_f. \tag{4.46}$$

Inserting (4.46) into the security market line (4.44) yields

$$0 = \beta_{\nu,t}^{(n)} \left(\mathbb{E}_t[R_{t+1}(\nu_t^{\text{ref}})] - r_f\right),$$

and consequently $\beta_{\nu,t}^{(n)} = 0$. If at least two risky assets are correlated and the prohibited short-selling constraint is binding such that $\langle e_n, \Sigma_t^{-1}\Pi_t\rangle < 0$, the expected excess return on the regulated asset appears *below* the straight line $\beta_{\nu,t}^{(n)} \left(\mathbb{E}_t[R_{t+1}(\nu_t^{\text{ref}})] - r_f\right)$. A similar observation can be found in LEVY (1983). The author considered a more general model with short-sale constraints on multiple risky assets, showing that there is linear relationship between average return and the systematic risk for assets which are included in the constrained-efficient reference portfolio. Moreover, the author showed that all securities with $x^{(i)} = 0$ appear below this straight line. However, a concrete formula describing the relationship between average return and beta was missing. Theorem 13 may be used to relate the expected excess return on a portfolio ω to the risk premium of ν_t^{ref}.

Corollary 3. *Let the hypothesis of Assumption 6 be satisfied. Then for each* $t \geq 0$ *the excess return on the portfolio* ω *satisfies*

$$\mathbb{E}_t[R_{t+1}(\omega)] - r_f = \begin{cases} \beta_{\nu,t}\left(\mathbb{E}_t[R_{t+1}(\nu_t^{\text{ref}})] - r_f\right) & \text{if } \langle e_n, \omega\rangle = 0, \\ \beta_{\nu,t}\left(\mathbb{E}_t[R_{t+1}(\nu_t^{\text{ref}})] - r_f\right) + \frac{\langle e_n, \Sigma_t^{-1}\Pi_t\rangle}{\langle e_n, \Sigma_t^{-1}e_n\rangle} & \text{if } \langle e_n, \omega\rangle \neq 0, \end{cases} \tag{4.47}$$

where

$$\beta_{\nu,t} := \frac{\mathbb{C}\text{ov}_t[R_{t+1}(\omega), R_{t+1}(\nu_t^{\text{ref}})]}{\mathbb{V}\text{ar}_t[R_{t+1}(\nu_t^{\text{ref}})]}. \tag{4.48}$$

The coefficient (4.48) at time t is referred to as the ν-*constrained beta coefficient of the portfolio* ω. Notice that the slope of the security market line is time-dependent and given by the expected excess return $\mathbb{E}_t[R_{t+1}(\nu_t^{\text{ref}})] - r_f$ of the benchmark portfolio ν_t^{ref}. According to Equation (4.47), the expected excess return on a portfolio with zero weights on the regulated asset, lies on the straight line $\beta_{\nu,t}\left(\mathbb{E}_t[R_{t+1}(\nu_t^{\text{ref}})] - r_f\right)$. This case is equivalent to the case of permitted short-selling on the smaller financial market with $n-1$ assets. If, however, a portfolio has non-zero weights on the regulated asset, then, since $\langle e_n, \Sigma_t^{-1}\Pi_t\rangle < 0$ the expected excess return on the portfolio lies *below* the security market line $\beta_{\nu,t}\left(\mathbb{E}_t[R_{t+1}(\nu_t^{\text{ref}})] - r_f\right)$.

In the preceding section we have shown that the beta coefficients capture the cross-sectional variability of the returns process $\{r_t\}_{t\geq 0}$. When short-selling is restricted, the security market line remains unchanged and the θ-constrained beta coefficient serves as a measure of systematic risk in the financial market. In a similar way, the ν-constrained beta coefficients can be used to decompose the total variance of a portfolio. Given a stochastic process of returns $\{r_t\}_{t\geq 0}$, one may choose a series of random variables $\{\varepsilon_t\}_{t\geq 0}$ such that the return on a portfolio $\omega \in \mathbb{R}^n$ satisfies

$$R_{t+1}(\omega) = r_f + \beta_{\nu,t}(R_{t+1}(\nu_t^{\text{ref}}) - r_f) + \varepsilon_{t+1} \tag{4.49}$$

for all $t \geq 0$. Corollary 3 implies that the expectations on the residual conditional on information available at time t is non-positive, satisfying

$$\mathbb{E}_t[\varepsilon_{t+1}] = \begin{cases} 0 & \text{if } \omega^{(n)} = 0, \\ \frac{\langle e_n, \Sigma_t^{-1}\Pi_t\rangle}{\langle e_n, \Sigma_t^{-1}e_n\rangle} < 0 & \text{otherwise.} \end{cases} \tag{4.50}$$

Equation (4.50) implies that a linear model to regress the portfolio return $R_{t+1}(\omega)$ on the reference return $R_{t+1}(\nu_t^*)$, will on average underestimate the risk premium $R_{t+1}(\omega) - r_f$ whenever $\omega^{(n)} \neq 0$. Taking the conditional covariance between $R_{t+1}(\omega)$ and $R_{t+1}(\nu_t^{\mathrm{ref}})$ and using the definition of the ν-constrained beta coefficient, yields

$$\mathbb{C}\mathrm{ov}_t[R_{t+1}(\omega), R_{t+1}(\nu_t^{\mathrm{ref}})] = \beta_{\nu,t}\mathbb{V}\mathrm{ar}_t[R_{t+1}(\nu_t^{\mathrm{ref}})] + \mathbb{C}\mathrm{ov}_t[\varepsilon_{t+1}, R_{t+1}(\nu_t^{\mathrm{ref}})] \tag{4.51}$$

$$= \mathbb{C}\mathrm{ov}_t[R_{t+1}(\omega), R_{t+1}(\nu_t^{\mathrm{ref}})]. \tag{4.52}$$

Thus, the residual is uncorrelated to the reference return $R_{t+1}(\nu_t^*)$, i.e.

$$\mathbb{C}\mathrm{ov}_t[\varepsilon_{t+1}, R_{t+1}(\nu_t^{\mathrm{ref}})] = 0.$$

The conditional variance of $R_{t+1}(\omega)$ is then given by

$$\begin{aligned}\mathbb{V}\mathrm{ar}[R_{t+1}(\omega)] &= (\beta_{\nu,t})^2\mathbb{V}\mathrm{ar}[R_{t+1}(\nu_t^{\mathrm{ref}})] + \mathbb{V}\mathrm{ar}[\varepsilon_{t+1}] + \mathbb{C}\mathrm{ov}_t[\varepsilon_{t+1}, R_{t+1}(\nu_t^{\mathrm{ref}})] \\ &= (\beta_{\nu,t})^2\mathbb{V}\mathrm{ar}[R_{t+1}(\nu_t^{\mathrm{ref}})] + \mathbb{V}\mathrm{ar}[\varepsilon_{t+1}]\end{aligned} \tag{4.53}$$

for all $t \geq 0$. In analogy to the unrestricted case, the first term in (4.53) is the *systematic risk* in period t and can be written as

$$(\beta_{\nu,t})^2\mathbb{V}\mathrm{ar}[R_{t+1}(\nu_t^{\mathrm{ref}})] = \mathbb{C}\mathrm{or}[R_{t+1}(\omega), R_{t+1}(\nu_t^{\mathrm{ref}})]^2\mathbb{V}\mathrm{ar}[R_{t+1}(\omega)]. \tag{4.54}$$

This risk cannot be reduced through diversification since every asset with non-zero beta contains this risk. The second term, the *non-systematic* risk in period t, can be formulated as

$$\mathbb{V}\mathrm{ar}[\varepsilon_{t+1}] = (1 - \mathbb{C}\mathrm{or}[R_{t+1}(\omega), R_{t+1}(\nu_t^{\mathrm{ref}})]^2)\mathbb{V}\mathrm{ar}[R_{t+1}(\omega)] \tag{4.55}$$

and is uncorrelated with ν_t^{ref}.

Conclusion

This thesis developed a comprehensive theoretical framework to study the consequences of short-sale constraints on the stability of financial markets. We considered investors with mean-variance preferences who seek to maximise utility by choosing an optimal portfolio which satisfies the enforced short-sale constraint. Establishing a generalised separation theorem, we decomposed the decision problem of finding an optimal portfolio into two parts: the multivariate value-maximising problem of finding a constrained-efficient portfolio and the univariate decision problem of determining the optimal risk. The constrained-efficient portfolio was shown to be mean-variance efficient in the frictionless market with $n-1$ risky assets, corrected by a portfolio which depends on the short-selling threshold. In particular, if a full ban on short-sales is set, the utility maximising portfolio was shown to be mean-variance efficient in the smaller asset market. Applying basic microeconomic principles, the risk-taking behaviour of an investor could be decomposed into an endowment and a price effect. Therefore, whether restricted short-selling will reduce the portfolio risk depends on the magnitudes of these effects. As short-sale constraints restrict the set of profitable investment opportunities, they may also adversely affect the default risk of investors. For elliptically distributed returns, we showed that a short-sale constraint lowers the default risk of an investor only if her portfolio risk is sufficiently reduced.

In Chapter 2, the consequences of short-sale constraints on equilibrium asset prices were analysed. Establishing existence and uniqueness of a CAPM equilibrium for a finite number of investors with heterogeneous beliefs, we contradicted the commonly hypothesised overpricing theory which states that short-sale constraints prevent a market decline by avoiding a precipitous downward spiral in prices. Our analysis showed that overpricing of securities is solely attributable to the subjective second moment beliefs of investors. The desired effect of an overpriced regulated stock occurs only if investors have low dispersion of beliefs, which in our model is embodied in the covariance matrix.

The static model was then embedded into a dynamic framework to analyse the evolution of asset prices and allocations in the long run. Numerical simu-

G. Hunanyan, *The Consequences of Short-Sale Constraints on the Stability of Financial Markets*, Finanzwirtschaft, Banken und Bankmanagement | Finance, Banks and Bank Management, https://doi.org/10.1007/978-3-658-27956-1_6

lations showed that, in addition to the subjective second moments, the noise traders' transactions determine whether the asset prices will be distorted upwards or downwards. Hence, limiting short-sales to prevent a market decline of asset prices, will in general miss its objective. Analysing price fluctuations, numerical results revealed that imposing short-sale constraints is not necessarily associated with a decrease in price volatility of the regulated asset. Nevertheless, the price process of the unregulated asset becomes slightly less volatile in the presence of short-selling limitations.

The thesis also analysed the effects of short-sale constraints on systematic risk, distinguishing between *prohibition* and *restriction* on short-sales. The risk-minimising investor was identified as the investor whose short-selling motive is diversification rather than profitability. We showed that both, prohibition and restriction on short-sales, reduce diversification possibilities leading to additional non-systematic risk. In order to analyse the effects of short-sale constraints on the entire financial market, we replaced the modified market portfolio from Wenzelburger (2018b) by constrained-efficient portfolios that satisfy the restricted and prohibited short-sale constraint, respectively. These portfolios are mean-variance efficient for any two consecutive trading periods and satisfy the respective short-sale constraint in period t. They attain the highest possible Sharpe ratio conditional on available information and their time-dependent beta coefficients allow to generalise the security market line to a time-dependent security market line for the regulated financial market. The beta coefficients thereby capture the full cross-sectional variability of a given returns process allowing a distinction between systematic and non-systematic risk in a dynamic setting.

In summary, the results of this thesis do not support the claim of the generally stabilising influence of short-sale constraints. It is important to note that in this thesis, only one asset was constrained while in a regulated financial market multiple assets may be restricted. Therefore, future research should consider the effect of short-sale constraints on a set of risky assets as well as on the risk-free bond.

From a dynamic perspective, two extensions of the presented model may be considered in future research: the introduction of investors with multiperiod planning horizons and the case with one expert agent, who is able to correctly forecast future prices. Due to tractability and its wide acceptance, we used standard deviation as a measure of investment risk. However, this measure of risk is criticised in finance literature as the possibility for large gains (upside volatility) contributes to a larger standard deviation. Therefore, a more challenging modification of this thesis would replace the standard deviation with the more meaningful *downside risk measure* for portfolio performance.

Appendix

A.1 Mathematical proofs

In this technical appendix, the proofs of all main results are collected.

Proofs of Section 1.2

Proof of Theorem 1. To solve the value-maximisation problem

$$\max_{x \in X} \mathrm{M}(x) \ \text{ s.t. } \ \mathrm{Sd}(x) \leq \sigma, \tag{A.1}$$

for the prescribed level of risk $\sigma \geq 0$, we establish existence and uniqueness of the solution before investigating its form. Note that if $\sigma = 0$, an investor will invest all of her initial wealth w_0 into the safe bond y. Thus, we consider the case $\sigma > 0$.

(i) Existence and Uniqueness: Uniqueness of the solution is guaranteed by the convexity of the set X of feasible portfolios and the linearity of the objective function. Since the objective function $\mathrm{M}(x)$ and the inequality constraints

$$\mathrm{Sd}(x) - \sigma \leq 0 \quad \text{and} \quad \chi - \langle e_n, x\rangle \leq 0,$$

are continuously differentiable and convex functions, the necessary Karush-Kuhn-Tucker (KKT) conditions are also sufficient. In other words, an optimal solution exists if and only if it satisfies the KKT conditions.

(ii) Form of the solution: The Lagrangian function of (A.1) is

$$\mathcal{L}(x, \lambda_1, \lambda_2) = R_f w_0 + \langle \pi, x\rangle + \lambda_1 \left(\sigma - \langle x, Vx\rangle^{\frac{1}{2}}\right) + \lambda_2[\langle e_n, x\rangle - \chi]$$

with $\sigma > 0$ and $\lambda_1, \lambda_2 \geq 0$. The first-order condition in vector form reads

$$V^{-1}(\pi + \lambda_2^* e_n) = \frac{\lambda_1^*}{\langle x^*, Vx^*\rangle^{\frac{1}{2}}} x^*, \tag{A.2}$$

G. Hunanyan, *The Consequences of Short-Sale Constraints on the Stability of Financial Markets*, Finanzwirtschaft, Banken und Bankmanagement | Finance, Banks and Bank Management, https://doi.org/10.1007/978-3-658-27956-1

where $e_n = (0, \ldots, 0, 1)^\top \in \mathbb{R}^n$ is the n-th canonical basis vector. The inverse matrix V^{-1} exists due to the positive definiteness of the covariance matrix V. The complementary slackness conditions are

$$\lambda_1^* \left(\sigma - \langle x^*, V x^* \rangle^{\frac{1}{2}} \right) = 0 \tag{A.3}$$

$$\lambda_2^* [\langle e_n, x^* \rangle - \chi] = 0. \tag{A.4}$$

Case 1: Suppose $\lambda_2^* = 0$ and $\lambda_1^* > 0$. Then $\sigma = \langle x^*, V x^* \rangle^{\frac{1}{2}}$ and the short-sale constraint is not binding. It follows from (A.2) and (A.3) that

$$x^* = \frac{\sigma}{\rho} V^{-1} \pi.$$

Inserting x^* into (A.4), we deduce that x^* is feasible if and only if

$$\sigma \leq \frac{\chi}{\langle e_n, \hat{x}_{\text{eff}} \rangle} =: \underline{\sigma}.$$

Case 2: Suppose $\lambda_2^* > 0$ and $\lambda_1^* > 0$. Then $x^* = \frac{\sigma}{\lambda_1^*} V^{-1} (\pi + \lambda_2^* e_n)$ and the complementary slackness conditions take the form of a non-linear system of equations

$$(\lambda_1^*)^2 = \langle \pi, V^{-1} \pi \rangle + 2\lambda_2^* \langle e_n, V^{-1} \pi \rangle + (\lambda_2^*)^2 \langle e_n, V^{-1} e_n \rangle \tag{A.5}$$

$$\chi = \frac{\sigma}{\lambda_1^*} \left(\langle e_n, V^{-1} \pi \rangle + \lambda_2^* \langle e_n, V^{-1} e_n \rangle \right). \tag{A.6}$$

Since the covariance matrix V and its inverse V^{-1} are positive definite, there exists a symmetric and positive definite matrix $B \in \mathbb{R}^{n \times n}$ such that $BB = V^{-1}$. The Cauchy-Schwarz inequality implies that

$$\langle e_n, V^{-1} \pi \rangle^2 = \langle B e_n, B \pi \rangle^2 \leq \langle B e_n, B e_n \rangle \langle B \pi, B \pi \rangle = \langle e_n, V^{-1} e_n \rangle \langle \pi, V^{-1} \pi \rangle, \tag{A.7}$$

where the inequality is strict whenever e_n and π are not collinear (or equivalently $\pi^{(k)} \neq 0$ for at least one asset $k \in \{1, \ldots, n-1\}$).

Case 2a: If short-selling is strictly forbidden, i.e. $\chi = 0$, Equation (A.6) implies that

$$\lambda_2^* = -\frac{\langle e_n, V^{-1} \pi \rangle}{\langle e_n, V^{-1} e_n \rangle}.$$

Inserting λ_2^* into (A.5) yields

$$\lambda_1^* = \left(\langle \pi, V^{-1} \pi \rangle - \frac{\langle e_n, V^{-1} \pi \rangle^2}{\langle e_n, V^{-1} e_n \rangle} \right)^{\frac{1}{2}} =: \underline{\rho}.$$

Thus, if $\chi = 0$, the constrained-efficient portfolio takes the form

$$x^* = \frac{\sigma}{\underline{\rho}}\left(V^{-1}\pi - \frac{\langle e_n, V^{-1}\pi\rangle}{\langle e_n, V^{-1}e_n\rangle}V^{-1}e_n\right). \tag{A.8}$$

<u>Case 2b:</u> Let $\chi < 0$. Then, dividing by χ and inserting (A.6) into (A.5) yields the quadratic equation

$$(\lambda_2^*)^2 + 2\frac{\langle e_n, V^{-1}\pi\rangle}{\langle e_n, V^{-1}e_n\rangle}\lambda_2^* + \frac{\frac{\sigma^2}{\chi^2}\langle e_n, V^{-1}\pi\rangle^2 - \langle \pi, V^{-1}\pi\rangle}{\frac{\sigma^2}{\chi^2}\langle e_n, V^{-1}e_n\rangle^2 - \langle e_n, V^{-1}e_n\rangle} = 0.$$

The only positive solution to this equation is

$$\lambda_2^* = -\frac{\langle e_n, V^{-1}\pi\rangle}{\langle e_n, V^{-1}e_n\rangle} + \frac{\underline{\rho}}{\sqrt{\frac{\sigma^2}{\chi^2}\langle e_n, V^{-1}e_n\rangle^2 - \langle e_n, V^{-1}e_n\rangle}}. \tag{A.9}$$

This solution is well-defined for all $\sigma \geq \underline{\sigma}$.[1] Inserting (A.9) into (A.6), the Lagrange multiplier λ_1^* becomes

$$\lambda_1^* = \frac{\underline{\rho}\sigma}{\sqrt{\sigma^2 - \frac{\chi^2}{\langle e_n, V^{-1}e_n\rangle}}}. \tag{A.10}$$

Thus, the maximisation problem (A.1) admits a unique solution which is given by

$$x_{\text{ceff}}(\sigma, \chi) = \begin{cases} \frac{\sigma}{\underline{\rho}}V^{-1}\pi & \text{if } \sigma \leq \underline{\sigma}, \\ \frac{\sqrt{\sigma^2 - \sigma_\chi^2}}{\underline{\rho}}\left(V^{-1}\pi - \frac{\langle e_n, V^{-1}\pi\rangle}{\langle e_n, V^{-1}e_n\rangle}V^{-1}e_n\right) + x_\chi & \text{if } \sigma > \underline{\sigma}, \end{cases} \tag{A.11}$$

where

$$x_\chi = \frac{\chi}{\langle e_n, V^{-1}e_n\rangle}V^{-1}e_n \quad \text{and} \quad \sigma_\chi = \mathrm{Sd}(x_\chi) = \frac{\chi}{\langle e_n, V^{-1}e_n\rangle^{\frac{1}{2}}}.$$

The expected final net worth is

$$\mathrm{M}(x_{\text{ceff}}(\sigma, \chi)) = \mathcal{E}(\sigma),$$

where $\mathcal{E}$ is given in (1.18). Observe that $\underline{\rho} = 0$ if $e_n = \alpha\pi$ for some $\alpha \in \mathbb{R}$, so that $\lambda_1^* = 0$. This, however, is ruled out.

---

[1] Equation (A.7) implies that $\frac{\langle \pi, V^{-1}\pi\rangle}{\langle e_n, V^{-1}\pi\rangle^2} > \frac{1}{\langle e_n, V^{-1}e_n\rangle}$. Hence, $\frac{\sigma^2}{\chi^2}\langle e_n, V^{-1}e_n\rangle^2 > \langle e_n, V^{-1}e_n\rangle$ if and only if $\sigma > \underline{\sigma}$.

Case 3: Suppose $\lambda_2^* = 0$ and $\lambda_1^* = 0$. Then (A.2) implies that $V^{-1}\pi = 0$. This case cannot occur, as $\pi \neq 0$ and V is invertible.

Summarising, we have shown that $x_{\text{ceff}}(\sigma, \chi)$, as given in (A.11), is the solution to (A.1) whenever $\pi \neq 0$. On the other hand, if $\pi^{(k)} = 0$ for all assets $k = 1, \dots, n$, we obtain $\text{Sd}(x) = 0$ for all x, implying that the solution must be $x_{\text{ceff}} = 0$.

It remains to show that

$$V^{-1}\pi - \frac{\langle e_n, V^{-1}\pi\rangle}{\langle e_n, V^{-1}e_n\rangle} V^{-1}e_n = \left(\begin{array}{c|c} (V_{\setminus n})^{-1} & \begin{matrix} 0 \\ \vdots \\ 0 \end{matrix} \\ \hline 0 \cdots 0 & 0 \end{array}\right) \pi,$$

where $V_{\setminus n}$ denotes the sub-matrix of V without the n-th column and n-th row. This is accomplished in three steps.

Step 1: Since $\langle e_n, V^{-1}\pi\rangle V^{-1}e_n = V^{-1}e_n\langle e_n, V^{-1}\pi\rangle = V^{-1}e_n e_n^\top V^{-1}\pi$, we conclude that

$$V^{-1}\pi - \frac{\langle e_n, V^{-1}\pi\rangle}{\langle e_n, V^{-1}e_n\rangle} V^{-1}e_n = \left(V^{-1} - \frac{1}{\langle e_n, V^{-1}e_n\rangle} V^{-1}e_n e_n^\top V^{-1}\right)\pi. \quad \text{(A.12)}$$

Step 2: Defining $W := V^{-1} - \frac{1}{\langle e_n, V^{-1}e_n\rangle} V^{-1}e_n e_n^\top V^{-1}$, the following holds true

$$\begin{aligned} We_n &= V^{-1}e_n - \frac{1}{\langle e_n, V^{-1}e_n\rangle} V^{-1}e_n e_n^\top V^{-1}e_n \\ &= V^{-1}e_n - \frac{\langle e_n, V^{-1}e_n\rangle}{\langle e_n, V^{-1}e_n\rangle} V^{-1}e_n \\ &= 0. \end{aligned}$$

Since V^{-1} is symmetric it follows

$$\begin{aligned} W^\top &= (V^{-1})^\top - \frac{1}{\langle e_n, V^{-1}e_n\rangle} (V^{-1})^\top e_n e_n^\top (V^{-1})^\top \\ &= V^{-1} - \frac{1}{\langle e_n, V^{-1}e_n\rangle} V^{-1}e_n e_n^\top V^{-1} = W, \end{aligned}$$

indicating that W is a symmetric matrix as well. Consequently, $e_n^\top W = (We_n)^\top = 0$, showing that the n-th column and n-th row of W is the zero vector.

Step 3: Finally, we want to prove that

$$W_{\setminus n} = \left(V^{-1} - \frac{1}{\langle e_n, V^{-1}e_n\rangle} V^{-1}e_n e_n^\top V^{-1}\right)_{\setminus n} = (V_{\setminus n})^{-1}.$$

To prove this claim we use the Schur-complement of $\langle e_n, V^{-1}e_n\rangle$ in the precision matrix V^{-1}. The covariance matrix V can be written as

$$V = (V^{-1})^{-1} = \left(\begin{array}{c|c} (V^{-1})_{\setminus n} & (V^{-1}e_n)_{\setminus n} \\ \hline (e^\top V^{-1})_{\setminus n} & \langle e_n, V^{-1}e_n\rangle \end{array}\right)^{-1},$$

and therefore

$$V_{\setminus n} = \left(\left(\begin{array}{c|c} (V^{-1})_{\setminus n} & (V^{-1}e_n)_{\setminus n} \\ \hline (e^\top V^{-1})_{\setminus n} & \langle e_n, V^{-1}e_n\rangle \end{array}\right)^{-1}\right)_{\setminus n}.$$

The block matrix inverse formula now yields

$$\begin{aligned}(V_{\setminus n})^{-1} &= (V^{-1})_{\setminus n} - \frac{1}{\langle e_n, V^{-1}e_n\rangle}(V^{-1}e_n)_{\setminus n}\left(e^\top V^{-1}\right)_{\setminus n} \\ &= \left(V^{-1} - \frac{1}{\langle e_n, V^{-1}e_n\rangle}V^{-1}e_n e_n^\top V^{-1}\right)_{\setminus n}.\end{aligned}$$

Summarising all three steps, we obtain

$$V^{-1}\pi - \frac{\langle e_n, V^{-1}\pi\rangle}{\langle e_n, V^{-1}e_n\rangle}V^{-1}e_n = W\pi$$

and thus,

$$\sqrt{\langle \pi, W\pi\rangle} = \sqrt{\langle \pi, V^{-1}\pi\rangle - \frac{\langle e_n, V^{-1}\pi\rangle^2}{\langle e_n, V^{-1}e_n\rangle}} = \underline{\rho}.$$

□

Proof of Theorem 2 (Separation theorem).
The proof of the Separation theorem is carried out in a step-by-step procedure. We will show that utility-maximising portfolios x^*, i.e. solutions to

$$\max_{x\in X} U(\mathrm{M}(x), \mathrm{Sd}(x)), \tag{A.13}$$

must be constrained-efficient, that is, they solve (A.1). Moreover, we show that in an interior optimum (μ^*, σ^*), the marginal rate of substitution between risk and return $S(\mu^*, \sigma^*)$ must be equal to the price of risk of the short-sale constraint $\mathcal{E}'(\sigma^*)$.

Note that if $S(\underline{\mu}, \underline{\sigma}) \geq \rho$, the constraint is not binding. A proof for this case is the classical one and may be found in WENZELBURGER (2010). We therefore assume that $S(\underline{\mu}, \underline{\sigma}) < \rho$.

Step 1 (Special Case): First, we examine the boundary case $\pi = 0$. WENZELBURGER (2010) showed that $x^* = 0$ is the unique solution to the unconstrained problem (1.5). Since $\langle e_n, x^* \rangle = 0 \geq \chi$, the portfolio $x^* = 0$ is feasible and hence optimal for the constrained problem (A.13). In this case the investor does not participate in the market for risky assets and the short-sale restriction is not binding. In the following we assume that $\pi \neq 0$.

Step 2 (Efficiency): We show that any solution $x^* \in X$ must be constrained-efficient. Suppose this is not the case. Then, by Theorem 1, a constrained-efficient portfolio $\hat{x} \in X$ exists with

$$\mathrm{M}(\hat{x}) > \mathrm{M}(x^*) \quad \text{and} \quad \mathrm{Sd}(\hat{x}) = \mathrm{Sd}(x^*).$$

Then Assumption 1 implies

$$U(\mathrm{M}(\hat{x}), \mathrm{Sd}(\hat{x})) > U(\mathrm{M}(x^*), \mathrm{Sd}(x^*)),$$

contradicting the optimality of x^*. Hence, if an optimal solution x^* exists, it must be constrained-efficient.

Step 3 (Equivalent 1-dimensional problem): For $x_{\text{ceff}} = x_{\text{ceff}}(\sigma, \chi)$ we have then

$$\mathrm{Sd}(x_{\text{ceff}}) = \sigma \quad \text{and} \quad \mathrm{M}(x_{\text{ceff}}) = \mathcal{E}(\sigma).$$

Inserting x_{ceff} into the objective function of (A.13) yields

$$U(\mathrm{M}(x_{\text{ceff}}), \mathrm{Sd}(x_{\text{ceff}})) = U(\mathcal{E}(\sigma), \sigma).$$

Hence, $x^* = x_{\text{ceff}}(\sigma^*, \chi)$ is a solution to the original optimisation problem (A.13), if and only if σ^* solves

$$\max_{\sigma \geq 0} U(\mathcal{E}(\sigma), \sigma). \tag{A.14}$$

Our next task is thus to show that there is a unique solution σ^* to (A.14).

Step 4 (Existence and uniqueness): To prove uniqueness, set

$$G(\sigma) := U(\mathcal{E}(\sigma), \sigma)$$

for $\sigma \geq \underline{\sigma}$. Assumption 1 ensures that U is strictly quasi-concave. Together with the concavity of $\mathcal{E}(\sigma)$, this yields the strict quasi-concavity of G, as

$$G(\lambda\sigma_1 + (1-\lambda)\sigma_2) > \min\{U(\mathcal{E}(\sigma_1), \sigma_1), U(\mathcal{E}(\sigma_2), \sigma_2)\} = \min\{G(\sigma_1), G(\sigma_2)\}$$

for $\lambda \in (0,1)$ and every $\sigma_1 \neq \sigma_2$ with $\sigma_1, \sigma_2 > \underline{\sigma}$. It is well known (see e.g. CAMBINI AND MARTEIN (2009)) that a strictly quasi-concave function $\sigma \mapsto G(\sigma)$ is either strictly decreasing on $[\underline{\sigma}, \infty)$ and strictly increasing on $[\underline{\sigma}, \infty)$ or attains its unique maximum in $\sigma^* > \underline{\sigma}$, while being strictly increasing on $[\underline{\sigma}, \sigma^*)$ and strictly decreasing on (σ^*, ∞). In particular, if a maximiser σ^* exists, it is uniquely determined. Hence, to establish existence, it suffices to show that G is non-increasing for all $\sigma \geq \underline{\sigma}$. Considering the derivative of G with respect to σ

$$G'(\sigma) = \mathcal{E}'(\sigma)\frac{\partial U}{\partial \mu}(\mathcal{E}(\sigma), \sigma) + \frac{\partial U}{\partial \sigma}(\mathcal{E}(\sigma), \sigma),$$

where $G'(\sigma) < 0$ if and only if $\mathcal{E}'(\sigma) < S(\mathcal{E}(\sigma), \sigma)$, we can distinguish between two cases:

- Let $G'(\underline{\sigma}) \leq 0$. Then $\mathcal{E}'(\underline{\sigma}) = \rho \leq S(\underline{\mu}, \underline{\sigma})$. This case is ruled out above as the short-sale constraint is not binding.
- Let $G'(\underline{\sigma}) > 0$. Since $\rho < \rho_U(\underline{\mu}, \underline{\sigma})$ and the indifference curve $I(\underline{\mu}, \underline{\sigma})$ is strictly convex, there exists $(\tilde{\mu}, \tilde{\sigma}) \in I(\underline{\mu}, \underline{\sigma})$ such that $\tilde{\mu} = \mathcal{E}(\tilde{\sigma}) > \underline{\mu}$ and

$$S(\underline{\mu}, \underline{\sigma}) < \mathcal{E}'(\underline{\sigma}) < S(\mathcal{E}(\tilde{\sigma}), \tilde{\sigma}).$$

  It follows that $G'(\underline{\sigma}) > 0 > G'(\tilde{\sigma})$ indicating that a solution to (A.14) exists.

□

Proofs of Section 1.4

Proof of Theorem 4. First, note that the coefficient of variation is independent of χ whenever the short-sale constraint is non-binding. Thus, $\mathrm{CV}_c'(\chi) = 0$ if $\varphi_c(\chi; w_0, \pi) < \underline{\sigma}$. We will therefore show that $\mathrm{CV}_c'(\chi) < 0$ if $\varphi_c(\chi; w_0, \pi) \geq \underline{\sigma}$. Using Euler's theorem we observe that

$$\mathcal{E}(\sigma, \chi) = \frac{\partial \mathcal{E}}{\partial \sigma}(\sigma, \chi)\sigma + \frac{\partial \mathcal{E}}{\partial \chi}(\sigma, \chi)\chi + R_f w_0. \tag{A.15}$$

Exploiting (A.15) and the concavity of $\mathcal{E}$ with respect to σ, we deduce that $\mathrm{CV}_c'(\chi) < 0$ if and only if

$$\varepsilon_{\varphi_c}(\chi) = \frac{\frac{\partial \varphi_c}{\partial \chi}(\chi; w_0, \pi)\chi}{\varphi_c(\chi; w_0, \pi)} > \frac{\frac{\partial \mathcal{E}}{\partial \chi}(\sigma_c, \chi)\chi}{\mathcal{E}(\sigma_c, \chi) - \frac{\partial \mathcal{E}}{\partial \sigma}(\sigma_c, \chi)\sigma_c} = \frac{\frac{\partial \mathcal{E}}{\partial \chi}(\sigma_c, \chi)\chi}{R_f w_0 + \frac{\partial \mathcal{E}}{\partial \chi}(\sigma_c, \chi)\chi}, \tag{A.16}$$

where $\sigma_c = \varphi_c(\chi; w_0, \pi)$. Since $\chi \leq 0$ and $\frac{\partial \mathcal{E}}{\partial \chi}(\sigma_c, \chi) < 0$ for all $\sigma \geq \underline{\sigma}$, the right hand side of (A.16) satisfies

$$0 \leq \frac{\frac{\partial \mathcal{E}}{\partial \chi}(\sigma, \chi)\chi}{R_f w_0 + \frac{\partial \mathcal{E}}{\partial \chi}(\sigma, \chi)\chi} < 1.$$

The claim now follows from (A.16). □

Proofs of Section 2.1

Proof of Theorem 5 . A CAPM equilibrium in the presence of the short-sale constraint consists of a price vector $p_{*c} \in \mathbb{R}^n$ and portfolio allocations $\phi_c^i \in \mathbb{R}^n$, $i = 1, \ldots, I$, such that

- at prices p_{*c} each allocation ϕ_c^i, $i = 1, \ldots, I$ is individually optimal and satisfies the short-sale constraint and
- the market of risky assets is cleared at prices p_{*c}, i.e.

$$\Phi_c(p; (\bar{q}^i, V^i)_{i=1}^I) := \sum_{i=1}^I \phi_c^i(p; \bar{q}^i, V^i) = x_{\mathrm{m}}, \tag{A.17}$$

  where $x_{\mathrm{m}} \in \mathbb{R}_+^n$ is the market portfolio.

Investors' preferences are given by the linear mean-variance utility function

$$U^i(\mu, \sigma) = \mu - \frac{1}{2a^i}\sigma^2, \tag{A.18}$$

where a^i, $i = 1, \ldots, I$ is the risk tolerance of the i-th investor. In Section 1.2 we showed that for *an arbitrary price vector* $p \in \mathbb{R}^n$, the portfolio allocation

$$\phi_c^i(p; \bar{q}^i, V^i) = \begin{cases} a^i(V^i)^{-1}(\bar{q}^i - R_f p) & \text{if } a^i\langle e_n, (V^i)^{-1}(\bar{q}^i - R_f p)\rangle \geq \chi, \\ a^i W^i(\bar{q}^i - R_f p) + x_\chi^i & \text{otherwise,} \end{cases} \tag{A.19}$$

with

$$x_\chi^i := \frac{\chi}{\langle e_n, (V^i)^{-1} e_n\rangle}(V^i)^{-1} e_n,$$

is individually optimal, satisfying the short-sale constraint. Since the portfolio allocation (A.19) is individually optimal for any price vector $p \in \mathbb{R}^n$, a unique CAPM equilibrium exists if and only if the equation

$$\sum_{i=1}^I \phi_c^i(p; \bar{q}^i, V^i) = x_{\mathrm{m}}, \tag{A.20}$$

attains a unique solution $p_{*c} \in \mathbb{R}^n$.

We prove existence and uniqueness in the single-asset case before generalising it to the n-asset case. If only one risky asset is traded, the portfolio allocation (A.19) simplifies to

$$\phi_c^i(p; \bar{q}^i, \mathrm{Var}^i(\tilde{q})) = \max\left\{\chi, \frac{a^i}{\mathrm{Var}^i(\tilde{q})}(\bar{q}^i - R_f p)\right\},$$

where $\phi_c^i(p; \bar{q}^i, \mathrm{Var}^i(\tilde{q})) > \chi$ if and only if

$$p < p_\chi^i := \frac{1}{R_f}\left(\bar{q}^i - \chi\frac{\mathrm{Var}^i(\tilde{q})}{a^i}\right).$$

Define $\mathfrak{V}_1 := \left[\max_i\{p_\chi^i\}, \infty\right) \subset \mathbb{R}$ as the set of all prices for which *all investors* violate the short-sale constraint (see Figure A.1). Then, the map

$$\Phi_c : \mathbb{R} \setminus \mathfrak{V}_1 \to \mathbb{R}_+ \quad \text{with} \quad p \mapsto \Phi_c(p) = \sum_{i=1}^{I} \phi_c^i(p; \bar{q}^i, \mathrm{Var}^i(\tilde{q}))$$

is a bijective function since Φ_c is strictly decreasing with $\mathrm{Im}(\Phi_c) = \mathbb{R}_+$, where $\mathrm{Im}(\Phi_c) = \{x \in \mathbb{R} \mid x = \Phi_c(p) \text{ for some } p \in \mathbb{R} \setminus \mathfrak{V}_1\}$ denotes the image of Φ_c. In particular, for all $x_{\mathrm{m}} \in \mathbb{R}_+$, there exists a subset of investors $\mathcal{J} \subsetneq \{1, \ldots, I\}$ and a unique price $p_{*c} \in \mathbb{R} \setminus \mathfrak{V}_1$ such that

$$\Phi_c(p_{*c}) = \sum_{i=1}^{I} \phi_c^i(p_{*c}; \bar{q}^i, \mathrm{Var}^i(\tilde{q})) = \sum_{i \notin \mathcal{J}} \chi + \sum_{i \in \mathcal{J}} \frac{a^i}{\mathrm{Var}^i(\tilde{q})}(\bar{q}^i - R_f p_{*c}) = x_{\mathrm{m}}.$$

The set $\mathcal{J}$ can be interpreted as the set of all long-sellers at the equilibrium asset prices. In Figure A.1 we observe that $\mathcal{J} = \{3\}$.

We are now proceeding with the n-asset case. For given beliefs $(\bar{q}^i, V^i)_{i=1}^I$, the set of all price vectors for which *all* investors violate the short-sale constraint is given by

$$\mathfrak{V}_n = \{p \in \mathbb{R}^n \mid a^i \langle e_n, (V^i)^{-1}(\bar{q}^i - R_f p)\rangle < \chi \;\forall i = 1, \ldots, I\}.$$

As in the single-asset case, a price vector $\dot{p} \in \mathfrak{V}_n$ cannot clear the market since the aggregate demand satisfies

$$\langle e_n, \sum_{i=1}^{I} \phi_c^i(\dot{p}; \bar{q}^i, V^i)\rangle = I\chi \leq 0,$$

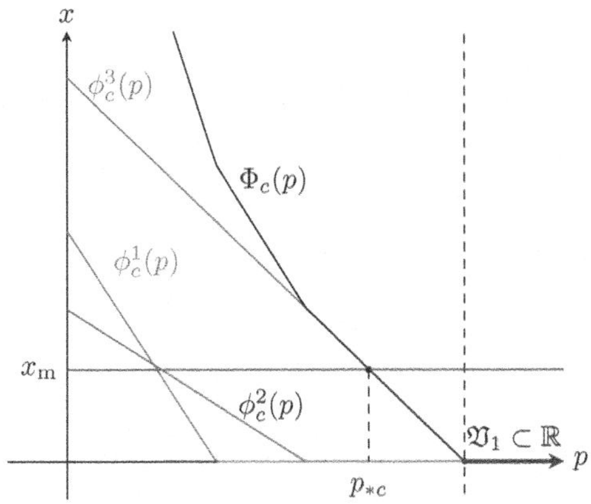

Figure A.1: The single-asset case

and the n-th risky asset is in positive net supply, i.e. $\langle e_n, x_m \rangle > 0$. Thus, if a solution to (A.20) exists, it lies in the complement of $\mathfrak{V}_n$, i.e.

$$\begin{aligned}\mathfrak{S}_n &:= \mathbb{R}^n \setminus \mathfrak{V}_n \\ &= \{p \in \mathbb{R}^n \mid \exists i = 1, \ldots, I \text{ with } a^i \langle e_n, (V^i)^{-1}(\bar{q}^i - R_f p)\rangle \geq \chi\}.\end{aligned}$$

The positive definiteness of V^i implies that for any $\bar{q}^i$ there exists a price vector $\hat{p} \in \mathbb{R}^n$ such that $a^i\langle e_n, (V^i)^{-1}(\bar{q}^i - R_f\hat{p})\rangle > \chi$. Thus $\hat{p} \in \mathfrak{S}_n$, showing that $\mathfrak{S}_n \neq \emptyset$ is non-empty. Again, due to the positive definiteness of at least one V^i, the map

$$\Phi_c : \mathfrak{S}_n \to \mathbb{R}^n_+ \quad \text{with} \quad p \mapsto \Phi_c(p) = \sum_{i=1}^{I} \phi_c^i(p; \bar{q}^i, V^i)$$

is a bijective function. Thus, for all $x_m \in \mathbb{R}^n$ there exists a price vector $p_{*c} \in \mathfrak{S}_n$ such that

$$\begin{aligned}\Phi_c(p_{*c}) &= \sum_{i=1}^{I} \phi_c^i(p_{*c}; \bar{q}^i, V^i) \\ &= \sum_{i \notin \mathcal{J}} (a^i W^i(\bar{q}^i - R_f p_{*c}) + x_\chi^i) + \sum_{i \in \mathcal{J}} a^i (V^i)^{-1}(\bar{q}^i - R_f p_{*c}) \qquad \text{(A.21)} \\ &= x_m.\end{aligned}$$

Rearranging (A.21) for the price vector p_{*c} yields

$$\sum_{i \notin \mathcal{J}} (a^i W^i \bar{q}^i + x_\chi^i) + \sum_{i \in \mathcal{J}} a^i (V^i)^{-1}\bar{q}^i - x_m = R_f \left(\sum_{i \notin \mathcal{J}} a^i W^i + \sum_{i \in \mathcal{J}} a^i (V^i)^{-1} \right) p_{*c},$$

where the coefficient matrix

$$\sum_{i \notin \mathcal{J}} a^i W^i + \sum_{i \in \mathcal{J}} a^i (V^i)^{-1}$$

is well-defined and invertible since W^i is positive semi-definite and V^i is positive definite. Therefore, a solution $p_{*c} \in \mathfrak{S}_n$ to (A.21) exists and is uniquely determined. The form of the solution, however, cannot be deduced as the subset $\mathcal{J}$ is not explicitly known. □

Proofs of Section 2.2

Proof of Theorem 7. Theorem 6 showed that

$$p_{*c} = \frac{1}{R_f} \left(\sum_{i=1}^{2} A_c^i \bar{q}^i - A_c \left(x_{\mathrm{m}} - x_{\chi}^1 \right) \right)$$

is the market clearing price vector whenever investor 1 is short-selling asset n at prices p_*. Inserting p_{*c} into (A.19), we obtain

$$\begin{aligned} x_{*c}^1 &= a^1 W^1 (\bar{q}^1 - R_f p_{*c}) + x_{\chi}^1 \\ &= a^1 W^1 \left(\bar{q}^1 - \sum_{i=1}^{2} A_c^i \bar{q}^i + A_c \left(x_{\mathrm{m}} - x_{\chi}^1 \right) \right) + x_{\chi}^1 \end{aligned}$$

and since $\sum_{i=1}^{2} A_c^i = \mathbb{1}_n$, where $\mathbb{1}_n$ is the identity matrix, the portfolio allocation x_{*c}^1 simplifies to

$$\begin{aligned} x_{*c}^1 &= a^1 W^1 \left(\bar{q}^1 - \sum_{i=1}^{2} A_c^i \bar{q}^i + A_c \left(x_{\mathrm{m}} - x_{\chi}^1 \right) \right) + x_{\chi}^1 \\ &= \sum_{i=1}^{2} B_c^{i1} (\bar{q}^1 - \bar{q}^i) + B_c^1 (x_{\mathrm{m}} - x_{\chi}^1) + x_{\chi}^1 \\ &= B_c^{21} (\bar{q}^1 - \bar{q}^2) + B_c^1 (x_{\mathrm{m}} - x_{\chi}^1) + x_{\chi}^1 \end{aligned}$$

where

$$B_c^1 = a^1 W^1 A_c \quad \text{and} \quad B_c^{21} = a^1 W^1 A_c^2 = a^2 B^1 (V^2)^{-1}.$$

Using an analogous reasoning, we obtain

$$\begin{aligned} x_{*c}^2 &= a^2(V^2)^{-1}\left(\bar{q}^2 - \sum_{i=1}^{2} A_c^i\bar{q}^i + A_c\left(x_{\mathrm{m}} - x_\chi^1\right)\right) \\ &= \sum_{i=1}^{2} B_c^{i2}(\bar{q}^2 - \bar{q}^i) + B_c^2(x_{\mathrm{m}} - x_\chi^1) \\ &= B_c^{12}(\bar{q}^2 - \bar{q}^1) + B_c^2(x_{\mathrm{m}} - x_\chi^1) \end{aligned}$$

where

$$B_c^2 = a^2(V^2)^{-1}A_c \quad \text{and} \quad B_c^{12} = a^2(V^2)^{-1}A_c^i = a^1 B_c^2 W^1.$$

□

Proof of Theorem 8. Let the hypothesis of Assumption 4 be satisfied. Then investor 1 short-sales asset n at the (unconstrained) equilibrium price vector

$$p_* = \frac{1}{R_f}A\left(a^1(V^1)^{-1}\bar{q}^1 + a^2(V^2)^{-1}\bar{q}^2 - x_{\mathrm{m}}\right). \tag{A.22}$$

where $A = \left(a^1(V^1)^{-1} + a^2(V^2)^{-1}\right)^{-1}$. Since $A\left(a^1(V^1)^{-1} + a^2(V^2)^{-1}\right) = \mathbb{1}_n$, we obtain

$$a^1A(V^1)^{-1} = \mathbb{1}_n - a^2A(V^2)^{-1}. \tag{A.23}$$

The unconstrained price vector then becomes

$$p_* = \frac{1}{R_f}\left(\bar{q}^1 + A(a^2(V^2)^{-1}(\bar{q}^2 - \bar{q}^1) - x_{\mathrm{m}})\right). \tag{A.24}$$

Since investor 1 is the short-seller of asset n at prices p_*, the constrained market clearing price vector is given by

$$p_{*c} = \frac{1}{R_f}A_c\left(a^1W^1\bar{q}^1 + a^2(V^2)^{-1}\bar{q}^2 - x_{\mathrm{m}} + x_\chi^1\right),$$

where $x_\chi^1 = \frac{\chi}{\langle e_n,(V^1)^{-1}e_n\rangle}(V^1)^{-1}e_n$ and $A_c = \left(a^1W^1 + a^2(V^2)^{-1}\right)^{-1}$. Using an analogous reasoning as above yields

$$p_{*c} = \frac{1}{R_f}\left(\bar{q}^1 + A_c\left(a^2(V^2)^{-1}(\bar{q}^2 - \bar{q}^1) - x_{\mathrm{m}} + x_\chi^1\right)\right). \tag{A.25}$$

Equation (A.24) can also be rewritten as

$$a^2(V^2)^{-1}(\bar{q}^2 - \bar{q}^1) - x_{\mathrm{m}} = A^{-1}(R_fp_* - \bar{q}^1). \tag{A.26}$$

Combining Equations (A.24), (A.25) and (A.26) yields

$$\begin{aligned} p_{*c} - p_* &= \frac{1}{R_f}\left((A_c - A)A^{-1}(R_f p_* - \bar{q}^1) + A_c x_\chi^1\right) \\ &= \frac{1}{R_f}\left((\mathbb{1}_n - A_c A^{-1})\pi_*^1 + A_c x_\chi^1\right), \end{aligned} \tag{A.27}$$

where $\pi_*^1 = \bar{q}^1 - R_f p_*$. Since

$$A_c(a^1 W^1 + a^2 (V^2)^{-1}) = \mathbb{1}_n \quad \text{and} \quad A^{-1} = (a^1 (V^1)^{-1} + a^2 (V^2)^{-1})$$

we conclude

$$(\mathbb{1}_n - A_c A^{-1})\pi_*^1 = a^1 A_c (W^1 \pi_*^1 - (V^1)^{-1}\pi_*^1) \tag{A.28}$$

$$= a^1 A_c \frac{\langle e_n, (V^1)^{-1}\pi_*^1\rangle}{\langle e_n, (V^1)^{-1} e_n\rangle}(V^1)^{-1} e_n. \tag{A.29}$$

The last equation follows as

$$W^1 \pi_*^1 = (V^1)^{-1}\pi_*^1 - \frac{\langle e_n, (V^1)^{-1}\pi_*^1\rangle}{\langle e_n, (V^1)^{-1} e_n\rangle}(V^1)^{-1} e_n. \tag{A.30}$$

Denoting the short-seller's unconstrained portfolio allocation at prices p_* by $\phi^1(p_*) = a^1 (V^1)^{-1}(q_1 - R_f p_*)$, we obtain

$$(\mathbb{1}_n - A_c A^{-1})\pi_*^1 = -\frac{\langle e_n, \phi^1(p_*)\rangle}{\langle e_n, (V^1)^{-1} e_n\rangle} A_c (V^1)^{-1} e_n. \tag{A.31}$$

Inserting (A.31) into (A.27), the price deviation becomes

$$p_{*c} - p_* = \frac{1}{R_f}\frac{\chi - \langle e_n, \phi^1(p_*)\rangle}{\langle e_n, (V^1)^{-1} e_n\rangle} A_c (V^1)^{-1} e_n.$$

□

Proof of Lemma 4. Let the hypothesis of Assumption 4 be satisfied and $n = 2$. Then, as shown in Example 7, the price of (the non-regulated) asset 1 will increase if and only if

$$\mathbb{C}\mathrm{ov}^2 \mathbb{V}\mathrm{ar}^1\left(\tilde{q}^{(1)}\right) > \mathbb{C}\mathrm{ov}^1 \mathbb{V}\mathrm{ar}^2\left(\tilde{q}^{(1)}\right), \tag{A.32}$$

where $\mathbb{C}\mathrm{ov}^i = \mathbb{C}\mathrm{ov}(\tilde{q}^{(1)}, \tilde{q}^{(2)})$. The price of the regulated asset, on the other hand, will increase if and only if

$$\frac{a^1}{a^2}\det V^2 + \mathbb{V}\mathrm{ar}^1\left(\tilde{q}^{(1)}\right)\mathbb{V}\mathrm{ar}^2\left(\tilde{q}^{(2)}\right) > \mathbb{C}\mathrm{ov}^2 \mathbb{C}\mathrm{ov}^1. \tag{A.33}$$

1. Let $\mathbb{C}\mathrm{ov}^1 \geq 0$ and $\mathbb{C}\mathrm{ov}^2 > 0$ and assume that the price of asset 1 increases. Then, Equation (A.32) implies that

$$\mathbb{V}\mathrm{ar}^1\left(\tilde{q}^{(1)}\right) > \frac{\mathbb{C}\mathrm{ov}^1}{\mathbb{C}\mathrm{ov}^2}\mathbb{V}\mathrm{ar}^2\left(\tilde{q}^{(1)}\right). \tag{A.34}$$

Inserting this inequality into (A.33) yields

$$\begin{aligned}\frac{a^1}{a^2}\det V^2 + \mathbb{V}\mathrm{ar}^1\left(\tilde{q}^{(1)}\right)\mathbb{V}\mathrm{ar}^2\left(\tilde{q}^{(2)}\right) &> \frac{a^1}{a^2}\det V^2 + \frac{\mathbb{C}\mathrm{ov}^1}{\mathbb{C}\mathrm{ov}^2}\mathbb{V}\mathrm{ar}^2\left(\tilde{q}^{(1)}\right)\mathbb{V}\mathrm{ar}^2\left(\tilde{q}^{(2)}\right)\\ &> \frac{\mathbb{C}\mathrm{ov}^1}{\mathbb{C}\mathrm{ov}^2}\mathbb{V}\mathrm{ar}^2\left(\tilde{q}^{(1)}\right)\mathbb{V}\mathrm{ar}^2\left(\tilde{q}^{(2)}\right)\\ &= \frac{\mathbb{C}\mathrm{ov}^1}{\mathbb{C}\mathrm{ov}^2}\left(\det V^2 + (\mathbb{C}\mathrm{ov}^2)^2\right) \geq \mathbb{C}\mathrm{ov}^1\mathbb{C}\mathrm{ov}^2.\end{aligned}$$

2. Let $\mathbb{C}\mathrm{ov}^1 \leq 0$ and $\mathbb{C}\mathrm{ov}^2 < 0$ and assume the price of asset 1 decreases. Then, Inequality (A.34) again holds, yielding (A.33).

□

Proof of Proposition 4. As shown in Theorem 8, the price deviation formula is given by

$$p_{*c} - p_* = \frac{1}{R_f}\frac{\chi - \langle e_n, \phi^1(p_*)\rangle}{\langle e_n, (V^1)^{-1}e_n\rangle}A_c(V^1)^{-1}e_n, \tag{A.35}$$

where $A_c = (a^1W^1 + a^2(V^2)^{-1})^{-1}$. Therefore, the asset price of security k increases if and only if

$$\langle e_k, A_c(V^1)^{-1}e_n\rangle > 0.$$

1. Let $V^1 = \gamma V^2$ for some $\gamma \in \mathbb{R}_+$ then,

$$\begin{aligned}(a^1W^1 + a^2(V^2)^{-1})^{-1}(V^1)^{-1} &= (a^1V^1W^1 + a^2V^1(V^2)^{-1})^{-1}\\ &= (a^1V^1W^1 + a^2\gamma\mathbb{1}_n)^{-1}.\end{aligned}$$

Since $W^1 = (V^1)^{-1} - \frac{1}{\langle e_n,(V^1)^{-1}e_n\rangle}(V^1)^{-1}e_ne_n^\top(V^1)^{-1}$,

$$V^1W^1 = \mathbb{1}_n - \frac{1}{\langle e_n, (V^1)^{-1}e_n\rangle}e_ne_n^\top(V^1)^{-1}$$

is as block matrix and can be written as

$$V^1W^1 = \begin{pmatrix} 1 & 0 & \dots & 0 & 0\\ 0 & 1 & \dots & 0 & 0\\ \vdots & 0 & \ddots & \vdots & 0\\ 0 & \dots & 0 & 1 & 0\\ d_{n,1} & \dots & d_{n,n-2} & d_{n,n-1} & 0\end{pmatrix}$$

for some $d_{n,1}, \dots d_{n,n-1} \in \mathbb{R}$. Consequently,

$$(a^1V^1W^1 + a^2\gamma\mathbb{1}_n)^{-1} = \begin{pmatrix} a^1+a^2\gamma & 0 & \dots & 0 & 0 \\ 0 & a^1+a^2\gamma & \dots & 0 & 0 \\ \vdots & 0 & \ddots & \vdots & 0 \\ 0 & \dots & 0 & a^1+a^2\gamma & 0 \\ d_{n,1} & \dots & d_{n,n-2} & d_{n,n-1} & a^2\gamma \end{pmatrix}^{-1}$$

$$= \begin{pmatrix} \frac{1}{a^1+a^2\gamma} & 0 & \dots & 0 & 0 \\ 0 & \frac{1}{a^1+a^2\gamma} & \dots & 0 & 0 \\ \vdots & 0 & \ddots & \vdots & 0 \\ 0 & \dots & 0 & \frac{1}{a^1+a^2\gamma} & 0 \\ l_{n,1} & \dots & l_{n,n-2} & l_{n,n-1} & \frac{1}{a^2\gamma} \end{pmatrix},$$

where $l_{n,k} = -\frac{d_{n,k}}{(a^1+a^2\gamma)a^2\gamma}$ for $k = 1, \dots, n-1$. Equation (A.35) thus implies $p_{*c} - p_* = (0, \dots, 0, \delta)^\top$, where

$$\delta = \frac{1}{R_f} \frac{\chi - \langle e_n, \phi^1(p_*)\rangle}{\langle e_n, (V^1)^{-1} e_n\rangle} \frac{1}{a^2\gamma} > 0.$$

2. If $\mathbb{C}\mathrm{ov}^i\left(\tilde{q}^{(k)}, \tilde{q}^{(n)}\right) = 0$ for $i = 1, 2$, and all $k = 1, \dots n-1$, the covariance matrix and the corresponding precision matrix can be written as

$$V^i = \left(\begin{array}{c|c} V^i_{\setminus n} & \begin{matrix} 0 \\ \vdots \\ 0 \end{matrix} \\ \hline 0 \cdots 0 & \mathbb{V}\mathrm{ar}^i(\tilde{q}^{(n)}) \end{array}\right), \quad (V^i)^{-1} = \left(\begin{array}{c|c} \left(V^i_{\setminus n}\right)^{-1} & \begin{matrix} 0 \\ \vdots \\ 0 \end{matrix} \\ \hline 0 \cdots 0 & \frac{1}{\mathbb{V}\mathrm{ar}^i(\tilde{q}^{(n)})} \end{array}\right) \quad \text{(A.36)}$$

for investors $i = 1, 2$, respectively. Consequently,

$$a^1V^1W^1 = a^1 \left(\begin{array}{c|c} \mathbb{1}_{n-1} & \begin{matrix} 0 \\ \vdots \\ 0 \end{matrix} \\ \hline 0 \cdots 0 & 0 \end{array}\right)$$

and

$$a^2V^1(V^2)^{-1} = a^2 \left(\begin{array}{c|c} V^1_{\setminus n}(V^2_{\setminus n})^{-1} & \begin{matrix} 0 \\ \vdots \\ 0 \end{matrix} \\ \hline 0 \cdots 0 & \frac{\mathbb{V}\mathrm{ar}^1(\tilde{q}^{(n)})}{\mathbb{V}\mathrm{ar}^2(\tilde{q}^{(n)})} \end{array}\right),$$

yielding

$$A_c(V^1)^{-1} = (a^1 V^1 W^1 + a^2 V^1 (V^2)^{-1})^{-1}$$

$$= \left(\begin{array}{c|c} a^1 \mathbb{1}_{n-1} + a^2 V^1_{\setminus n} (V^2_{\setminus n})^{-1} & \begin{matrix} 0 \\ \vdots \\ 0 \end{matrix} \\ \hline 0 \cdots 0 & \frac{\mathbb{V}\mathrm{ar}^1(\tilde{q}^{(n)})}{\mathbb{V}\mathrm{ar}^2(\tilde{q}^{(n)})} \end{array} \right)^{-1}. \tag{A.37}$$

Inserting (A.37) into the price deviation formula (A.35) implies that $p_{*c} - p_* = (0, \dots, 0, \zeta)^\top$, where

$$\zeta = \frac{1}{R_f} \frac{\chi - \langle e_n, \phi^1(p_*) \rangle}{\mathbb{V}\mathrm{ar}^2(\tilde{q}^{(n)})} > 0.$$

□

Proofs of Section 4.1

Some proofs in this section require the explicit form of the risk-minimising portfolio, i.e. the solution of the decision problem

$$\min_{\omega \in \mathbb{R}^n} \mathbb{V}\mathrm{ar}_t[R_{t+1}(\omega)] \text{ s.t. } \mathbb{E}_t[R_{t+1}(\omega)] \geq \mu \text{ and } \langle e_n, \omega \rangle \geq \xi. \tag{A.38}$$

To ensure the existence and uniqueness of the constrained-efficient portfolio we consider a return process such that market participation takes places on the smaller financial market.

Assumption A.1. *Let $\{r_t\}_{t \geq 0}$ be a return process of n risky assets such that $\langle e_k, \Pi_t \rangle \neq 0$ for at least one risky asset $k \neq n$.*

The following proposition characterises the constrained-efficient portfolios.

Proposition A.1. *Let the hypotheses of Assumptions 6 and A.1 be satisfied. Setting $\underline{\mu}_t := r_f + \xi \frac{\langle \Pi_t, \Sigma_t^{-1} \Pi_t \rangle}{\langle e_n, \Sigma_t^{-1} \Pi_t \rangle}$, the optimisation problem (A.38) admits a unique solution which takes the form*

$$\omega^*_{c,t}(\mu, \xi) = \begin{cases} \frac{\mu - r_f}{\langle \Pi_t, \Sigma_t^{-1} \Pi_t \rangle} \Sigma_t^{-1} \Pi_t & \text{if } \mu \leq \underline{\mu}_t, \\ \frac{\mu - \mu_t^\xi}{\langle \Pi_t, \Omega_t \Pi_t \rangle} \Omega_t \Pi_t + \frac{\xi}{\langle e_n, \Sigma_t^{-1} e_n \rangle} \Sigma_t^{-1} e_n & \text{if } \mu > \underline{\mu}_t, \end{cases} \tag{A.39}$$

where $\mu_t^\xi = r_f + \xi \frac{\langle e_n, \Sigma_t^{-1} \Pi_t \rangle}{\langle e_n, \Sigma_t^{-1} e_n \rangle}$ and $\Omega_t := \left(\begin{array}{c|c} (\Sigma_{t \setminus n})^{-1} & \begin{matrix} 0 \\ \vdots \\ 0 \end{matrix} \\ \hline 0 \cdots 0 & 0 \end{array} \right)$ with $(\Sigma_{t \setminus n})^{-1}$ being the covariance matrix on the smaller security market. Moreover, if $\Pi_t = 0$ then $\omega^*_{c,t}(\mu, \xi) = 0$.

Proof. To solve the risk-minimisation problem (A.38), we establish existence and uniqueness of a solution before investigating its form. Note that if $\mu \leq r_f$ an investor will invest all of her initial wealth into the safe bond. Therefore, we assume $\mu > r_f$.
(i) Existence and Uniqueness: Since the objective function $\mathbb{V}\mathrm{ar}_t[R_{t+1}(\omega)]$ and the constraints

$$\mathbb{E}_t[R_{t+1}(\omega)] \geq \mu \quad \text{and} \quad \langle e_n, \omega \rangle \geq \xi$$

are continuously differentiable convex functions, the necessary Karush-Kuhn-Tucker (KKT) conditions are also sufficient. Uniqueness of the solution is guaranteed by the convexity of the objective function and the linearity of the constraints. Therefore, an optimal solution exists if and only if it satisfies the KKT conditions.
(ii) Form of the solution: The Lagrangian function of (A.38) is

$$\mathcal{L}(\omega, \lambda_1, \lambda_2) = -\frac{1}{2}\langle \omega, \Sigma_t \omega \rangle + \lambda_1[\langle \Pi_t, \omega \rangle - \Delta\mu] + \lambda_2[\langle e_n, \omega \rangle - \xi]$$

where $\Delta\mu := \mu - r_f > 0$ and $\lambda_1, \lambda_2 \geq 0$. At time t, the first-order condition in vector form reads

$$\omega^*_{c,t} = \Sigma_t^{-1}\left[\lambda^*_{1,t}\Pi_t + \lambda^*_{2,t} e_n\right]. \tag{A.40}$$

The inverse matrix Σ_t^{-1} exists due to the positive definiteness of the covariance matrix Σ_t. The complementary slackness conditions are

$$\lambda^*_{1,t}[\Delta\mu - \langle \Pi_t, \omega^*_{c,t} \rangle] = 0 \tag{A.41}$$
$$\lambda^*_{2,t}[\xi - \langle e_n, \omega^*_{c,t} \rangle] = 0. \tag{A.42}$$

Case 1: Suppose $\lambda^*_{2,t} = 0$ and $\lambda^*_{1,t} > 0$. Then, $\lambda^*_{1,t} = \frac{\Delta\mu}{\langle \Pi_t, \Sigma_t^{-1}\Pi_t \rangle}$ and the short-sale constraint is not binding. From (A.40) we obtain

$$\omega^*_{c,t} = \frac{\mu - r_f}{\langle \Pi_t, \Sigma_t^{-1}\Pi_t \rangle}\Sigma_t^{-1}\Pi_t.$$

Inserting $\omega^*_{c,t}$ into (A.42), we deduce that $\omega^*_{c,t}$ is feasible if and only if

$$\mu \leq \underline{\mu}_t = r_f + \xi\frac{\langle \Pi_t, \Sigma_t^{-1}\Pi_t \rangle}{\langle e_n, \Sigma_t^{-1}\Pi_t \rangle}.$$

Case 2: Suppose $\lambda^*_{2,t} > 0$ and $\lambda^*_{1,t} > 0$, then $\omega^*_{c,t} = \Sigma_t^{-1}\left[\lambda^*_{1,t}\Pi_t + \lambda^*_{2,t}e_n\right]$ and the complementary slackness conditions yield the following system of linear equations

$$\begin{aligned} \langle \Pi_t, \Sigma_t^{-1}\Pi_t \rangle \lambda^*_{1,t} + \langle e_n, \Sigma_t^{-1}\Pi_t \rangle \lambda^*_{2,t} &= \Delta\mu \\ \langle e_n, \Sigma_t^{-1}\Pi_t \rangle \lambda^*_{1,t} + \langle e_n, \Sigma_t^{-1}e_n \rangle \lambda^*_{2,t} &= \xi. \end{aligned} \tag{A.43}$$

The Cauchy-Schwarz inequality and the positive definiteness of Σ_t imply that the determinant D_t of the system (A.43) satisfies

$$D_t = \left\langle \Pi_t, \Sigma_t^{-1}\Pi_t \right\rangle \left\langle e_n, \Sigma_t^{-1} e_n \right\rangle - \left\langle e_n, \Sigma_t^{-1}\Pi_t \right\rangle^2 \geq 0.$$

Note that the inequality is strict if and only if there is at least one asset k such that $\langle e_k, \Pi_t \rangle \neq 0$. Hence, if the hypothesis of Assumption A.1 is satisfied, $D_t > 0$. Using Cramer's rule, the Lagrange multipliers take the form

$$\begin{pmatrix} \lambda_{1,t}^* \\ \lambda_{2,t}^* \end{pmatrix} = \frac{1}{D_t} \begin{pmatrix} \langle e_n, \Sigma_t^{-1} e_n \rangle & -\langle e_n, \Sigma_t^{-1}\Pi_t \rangle \\ -\langle e_n, \Sigma_t^{-1}\Pi_t \rangle & \langle \Pi_t, \Sigma_t^{-1}\Pi_t \rangle \end{pmatrix} \begin{pmatrix} \Delta\mu \\ \xi \end{pmatrix}, \tag{A.44}$$

and are well-defined for all $\mu \geq \underline{\mu}_t$. Inserting (A.44) into (A.40) and rearranging yields

$$\omega_{c,t}^*(\mu, \xi) = \begin{cases} \frac{\mu - r_f}{\langle \Pi_t, \Sigma_t^{-1}\Pi_t \rangle} \Sigma_t^{-1}\Pi_t & \text{if } \mu \leq \underline{\mu} \\ \frac{\mu - \mu_t^\xi}{\langle \Pi_t, \Omega_t \Pi_t \rangle} \left(\Sigma_t^{-1}\Pi_t - \frac{\langle e_n, \Sigma_t^{-1}\Pi_t \rangle}{\langle e_n, \Sigma_t^{-1} e_n \rangle} \Sigma_t^{-1} e_n \right) + \frac{\xi}{\langle e_n, \Sigma_t^{-1} e_n \rangle} \Sigma_t^{-1} e_n & \text{if } \mu > \underline{\mu}, \end{cases}$$

where $\mu_t^\xi = r_f + \xi \frac{\langle e_n, \Sigma_t^{-1}\Pi_t \rangle}{\langle e_n, \Sigma_t^{-1} e_n \rangle}$. The partitioning technique used in Appendix A.1 implies

$$\Sigma_t^{-1}\Pi_t - \frac{\langle e_n, \Sigma_t^{-1}\Pi_t \rangle}{\langle e_n, \Sigma_t^{-1} e_n \rangle} \Sigma_t^{-1} e_n = \Omega_t \Pi_t.$$

Case 3: Suppose $\lambda_{2,t}^* = 0$ and $\lambda_{1,t}^* = 0$. Then Equation (A.40) implies that $\Sigma_t^{-1}\Pi_t = 0$. This case cannot occur as it is contrary to $\Pi_t \neq 0$ and Σ_t invertible.

Summarising, we have shown that $\omega_{c,t}^*(\mu, \xi)$ is the solution to (A.38) whenever $\Pi_t \neq 0$. If $\langle e_k, \Pi_t \rangle = 0$ for all assets $k = 1, \ldots, n$, we obtain $\mathbb{E}_t[R_{t+1}(\omega)] = r_f$ for all ω, implying that the solution must be the zero vector 0. □

Inserting the constrained-efficient portfolio weights into the objective function $\mathbb{V}\mathrm{ar}_t[R_{t+1}(\omega)]$ and denoting $\underline{\rho}_t = \langle \Pi_t, \Omega_t \Pi_t \rangle^{\frac{1}{2}}$ as the conditional price of risk on the smaller financial market, we obtain the constrained-capital allocation curve

$$C_t(\sigma) = \begin{cases} r_f + \rho_t \sigma & \text{if } \sigma \leq \frac{\xi}{\langle e_n, \Sigma_t^{-1}\Pi_t \rangle}, \\ \mu_t^\xi + \underline{\rho}_t \sqrt{\sigma^2 - (\sigma_t^\xi)^2} & \text{otherwise}, \end{cases} \tag{A.45}$$

where $\sigma_t^\xi = \frac{\xi}{\sqrt{\langle e_n, \Sigma_t^{-1} e_n \rangle}}$.

Proof of Proposition 8. Let $\{r_t\}_{t \geq 0}$ be a return process of n risky assets such that the hypothesis of Assumption 6 is satisfied. The Sharpe ratio of the portfolio return $R_{t+1}(\omega)$ on $\omega \in \mathbb{R}$ conditional on information available in period t is formally given by

$$\mathrm{SR}_t(\omega) := \frac{\mathbb{E}_t[R_{t+1}(\omega)] - r_f}{\sqrt{\mathbb{V}\mathrm{ar}_t[R_{t+1}(\omega)]}} = \frac{\langle \Pi_t, \omega \rangle}{\sqrt{\langle \omega, \Sigma_t \omega \rangle}}. \tag{A.46}$$

First, we show that portfolios that maximise the Sharpe ratio are constrained-efficient. Suppose this is not the case and let $\hat{\omega}$ be an inefficient portfolio with $\mathrm{SR}(\hat{\omega}) = \rho$. Then, by Proposition A.1, there exists a constrained-efficient portfolio ω^* such that

$$\mathbb{E}_t[R_{t+1}(\omega^*)] = \mathbb{E}_t[R_{t+1}(\hat{\omega})] \quad \text{and} \quad \sqrt{\mathbb{V}\mathrm{ar}_t[R_{t+1}(\omega^*)]} < \sqrt{\mathbb{V}\mathrm{ar}_t[R_{t+1}(\hat{\omega})]},$$

or

$$\mathbb{E}_t[R_{t+1}(\omega^*)] > \mathbb{E}_t[R_{t+1}(\hat{\omega})] \quad \text{and} \quad \sqrt{\mathbb{V}\mathrm{ar}_t[R_{t+1}(\omega^*)]} = \sqrt{\mathbb{V}\mathrm{ar}_t[R_{t+1}(\hat{\omega})]}.$$

In both cases, $\mathrm{SR}_t(\omega^*) > \mathrm{SR}_t(\hat{\omega})$ contradicting $\mathrm{SR}(\hat{\omega}) = \rho$. Inserting the constrained-efficient portfolio (A.39) into (A.46), we obtain

$$\mathrm{SR}(\omega^*_{c,t}(\mu)) = \frac{\frac{\langle e_n, \Sigma_t^{-1} \Pi_t \rangle}{\langle e_n, \Sigma_t^{-1} e_n \rangle} \xi + \underline{\rho}_t \sqrt{\mathbb{V}\mathrm{ar}_t[R_{t+1}(\omega^*_{c,t}(\mu))] - (\sigma_t^{\xi})^2}}{\sqrt{\mathbb{V}\mathrm{ar}_t[R_{t+1}(\omega^*_{c,t}(\mu))]}} \tag{A.47}$$

if $\mu > \underline{\mu}_t$ and $\mathrm{SR}(\omega^*_{c,t}(\mu)) = \rho_t$ if $r_f < \mu \leq \underline{\mu}_t$. The concavity of C_t implies that

$$\frac{\frac{\langle e_n, \Sigma_t^{-1} \Pi_t \rangle}{\langle e_n, \Sigma_t^{-1} e_n \rangle} \xi + \underline{\rho}_t \sqrt{\mathbb{V}\mathrm{ar}_t[R_{t+1}(\omega^*_{c,t}(\mu))] - (\sigma_t^{\xi})^2}}{\sqrt{\mathbb{V}\mathrm{ar}_t[R_{t+1}(\omega^*_{c,t}(\mu))]}} < \rho_t$$

for all $\mu > \underline{\mu}_t$. Therefore, if short-selling is restricted, the portfolio weights $\omega^*_{c,t}(\mu)$ with $r_f < \mu \leq \underline{\mu}$ attain the highest possible Sharpe ratio ρ_t. If short-selling is prohibited any $\omega^*_{c,t} = \lambda \Omega_t \Pi_t$ with $\lambda > 0$ maximises (A.46) and the highest Sharpe ratio is given by $\underline{\rho}$. □

Proofs of Section 4.2

Proof of Theorem 10. Let $\{r_t\}_{t \geq 0}$ be a stochastic return process of n risky assets that meets the hypotheses of Assumptions 6 and A.1. Denote the period-$t{+}1$ wealth of an investor holding the portfolio ω by $\tilde{w}_{t+1}(\omega)$. Then the default probability associated with the portfolio $\omega \in \mathbb{R}$ is given by

$$\mathrm{Prob}(\tilde{w}_{t+1}(\omega) < 0) = \mathrm{Prob}\left(\frac{\tilde{w}_{t+1}(\omega) - \mathbb{E}_t[R_{t+1}(\omega)]}{\sqrt{\mathbb{V}\mathrm{ar}_t[R_{t+1}(\omega)]}} < -\frac{\mathbb{E}_t[R_{t+1}(\omega)]}{\sqrt{\mathbb{V}\mathrm{ar}_t[R_{t+1}(\omega)]}} \right).$$

HUNANYAN AND WENZELBURGER (2018A) showed that the default probability of a mean-variance efficient investor increases in the coefficient of variation of future wealth, provided that the return process is elliptically distributed. WENZELBURGER (2018A) extended this result by showing that the default risk associated with portfolios that have the same portfolio mix decreases in the coefficient of variation independently of the distributional assumption.[2] □

Proofs of Section 4.3

Proof of Theorem 13. Consider a return process of n risky assets which satisfies the hypothesis of Assumptions 6 with $\langle e_n, \omega_t^{\mathrm{ref}}\rangle > 0$ at time t. Then the short-sale constraint is non-binding and the reference portfolio ω_t^{ref} given in WENZELBURGER (2018B) is well-defined in the presence of prohibited short-selling as well. Suppose therefore $\langle e_n, \omega_t^{\mathrm{ref}}\rangle < 0$. The ν-constrained reference portfolio is then given by

$$\nu_t^{\mathrm{ref}} = \frac{1}{\sqrt{\langle \Pi_t, \Omega_t \Pi_t\rangle}} \Omega_t \Pi_t = \frac{1}{\sqrt{\langle \Pi_t, \Omega_t \Pi_t\rangle}} \left(\Sigma_t^{-1}\Pi_t - \frac{\langle e_n, \Sigma_t^{-1}\Pi_t\rangle}{\langle e_n, \Sigma_t^{-1} e_n\rangle} \Sigma_t^{-1} e_n \right).$$

Reformulating the above equation we obtain

$$\begin{aligned} \Pi_t &= \sqrt{\langle \Pi_t, \Omega_t \Pi_t\rangle}\, \Sigma_t \nu_t^{\mathrm{ref}} + \frac{\langle e_n, \Sigma_t^{-1}\Pi_t\rangle}{\langle e_n, \Sigma_t^{-1} e_n\rangle} e_n \\ &= \frac{\mathbb{E}_t[R_{t+1}(\nu_t^{\mathrm{ref}})] - r_f}{\mathbb{V}\mathrm{ar}_t[R_{t+1}(\nu_t^{\mathrm{ref}})]} \Sigma_t \nu_t^{\mathrm{ref}} + \frac{\langle e_n, \Sigma_t^{-1}\Pi_t\rangle}{\langle e_n, \Sigma_t^{-1} e_n\rangle} e_n, \end{aligned} \tag{A.48}$$

where the last equation holds due to Proposition 8 and $\sqrt{\mathbb{V}\mathrm{ar}_t[R_{t+1}(\nu_t^{\mathrm{ref}})]} = 1 = \mathbb{V}\mathrm{ar}_t[R_{t+1}(\nu_t^{\mathrm{ref}})]$. Taking the k-th component in (A.48) and using the relations

$$\langle e_k, \Sigma_t \nu_t^{\mathrm{ref}}\rangle = \mathbb{C}\mathrm{ov}_t[r_{t+1}^{(k)}, R_{t+1}(\nu_t^{\mathrm{ref}})] \quad \text{and} \quad \langle e_k, e_n\rangle = \begin{cases} 0 & \text{if } k \neq n, \\ 1 & \text{if } k = n, \end{cases}$$

completes the proof. □

[2] If $\omega = \lambda \Sigma_t^{-1}\Pi_t$ with $\lambda \in \mathbb{R}_+$ be a mean-variance efficient portfolio, then

$$\frac{\tilde{w}_{t+1}(\omega) - \mathbb{E}_t[R_{t+1}(\omega)]}{\sqrt{\mathbb{V}\mathrm{ar}_t[R_{t+1}(\omega)]}} = \frac{\langle \tilde{\Pi}_t - \Pi_t, \omega\rangle}{\sqrt{\mathbb{V}\mathrm{ar}_t[R_{t+1}(\omega)]}} = \langle \tilde{\Pi}_t - \Pi_t, \Sigma_t \Pi_t\rangle.$$

Therefore, the normalised future wealth has the same distribution as the return process.

Proof of Corollary 3. Using Theorem 13, we can compute the conditional expected excess return on ω by

$$\begin{aligned}\mathbb{E}_t[R_{t+1}(\omega)] - r_f &= \sum_{k=1}^{n} \omega^{(k)} \left(\mathbb{E}_t[r_{t+1}^{(k)}] - r_f\right) \\ &= \sum_{k=1}^{n} \langle e_k, \omega\rangle \frac{\mathbb{C}\mathrm{ov}_t[r_{t+1}^{(k)}, R_{t+1}(\nu_t^{\mathrm{ref}})]}{\mathbb{V}\mathrm{ar}_t[R_{t+1}(\nu_t^{\mathrm{ref}})]} \left(\mathbb{E}_t[R_{t+1}(\nu_t^{\mathrm{ref}})] - r_f\right) \\ &+ \frac{\langle e_n, \Sigma_t^{-1}\Pi_t\rangle}{\langle e_n, \Sigma_t^{-1} e_n\rangle},\end{aligned}$$

where

$$\sum_{k=1}^{n} \langle e_k, \omega\rangle \frac{\mathbb{C}\mathrm{ov}_t[r_{t+1}^{(k)}, R_{t+1}(\nu_t^{\mathrm{ref}})]}{\mathbb{V}\mathrm{ar}_t[R_{t+1}(\nu_t^{\mathrm{ref}})]} = \frac{\mathbb{C}\mathrm{ov}_t[R_{t+1}(\omega), R_{t+1}(\nu_t^{\mathrm{ref}})]}{\mathbb{V}\mathrm{ar}_t[R_{t+1}(\nu_t^{\mathrm{ref}})]} = \beta_{\nu,t}.$$

□

A.2 Minimum-variance portfolio

To solve the risk-minimisation problem

$$\min_{x \in \mathbb{R}^n} \mathrm{Sd}(x) \quad \text{s.t.} \quad \langle e_n, x\rangle = \chi \tag{A.49}$$

we first prove existence and uniqueness of the solution before analysing its form.

(i) Existence and Uniqueness: Using an analogous reasoning as in the proof of Theorem 1, we conclude that the Karush-Kuhn-Tucker (KKT) condition are also sufficient.

(ii) Form of the solution: The Lagrangian function of (A.49) is given by

$$\mathcal{L}(x, \lambda_1, \lambda_2) = -\langle x, Vx\rangle^{\frac{1}{2}} + \lambda[\chi - \langle e_n, x\rangle]$$

with $\lambda \geq 0$. The first-order condition in vector form reads

$$x_\chi = -\lambda^* V^{-1} e_n. \tag{A.50}$$

Thus, the risk-minimising portfolio x^* satisfies the short-sale constraint if and only if

$$-\lambda^* \langle e_n, V^{-1} e_n\rangle = \chi. \tag{A.51}$$

Consequently, $\lambda^* = -\frac{\chi}{\langle e_n, V^{-1}e_n\rangle}$ and the minimum-variance portfolio becomes

$$x_\chi = \frac{\chi}{\langle e_n, V^{-1}e_n\rangle} V^{-1}e_n. \tag{A.52}$$

Note that, if short-selling is prohibited, i.e. $\chi = 0$ then $x_\chi = 0$ and an investor will invest all of her initial wealth w_0 into the safe bond y.

In the following we show that the minimum-variance portfolio can be used to derive a direct characterisation of the precision matrix, i.e. the inverse of covariance matrix.[3] The k-th entry in the n-th row of the precision matrix can be written as

$$\langle e_k, V^{-1}e_n\rangle = \langle e_n, V^{-1}e_n\rangle \frac{x_\chi^{(k)}}{\chi}. \tag{A.53}$$

Using, Equation (A.53), we can construct the entries (k, l) of the precision matrix by determining the minimum-variance portfolio in the presence of the restricted short-selling constraints $\langle e_l, x\rangle \geq \chi$ of all asset $l = 1, \ldots, n$.

STEVENS (1998) showed that the n-th diagonal entry of the precision matrix can be represented as

$$\langle e_n, V^{-1}e_n\rangle = \left(\mathbb{V}\mathrm{ar}(\tilde{q}^{(n)})(1 - R_n^2)\right)^{-1},$$

where $0 \leq R_n^2 < 1$ is the *multiple regression coefficient* for regressing the return on asset n from those of all other assets. For example, if the investor expects the assets to be uncorrelated then $R_n^2 = 0$ and $\langle e_n, V^{-1}e_n\rangle = (\mathbb{V}\mathrm{ar}(\tilde{q}^{(n)}))^{-1}$. Therefore, the term $\mathbb{V}\mathrm{ar}(\tilde{q}^{(n)})(1 - R_n^2)$ is interpreted as the *residual variance* of asset n (see e.g. ANDERSON AND DANTHINE (1981)). We show in the following proposition that the demand of each asset in both, the efficient as well as the constrained-efficient portfolio with unit risk, is bounded by the *inverse residual standard deviation* of its return.

Proposition A.2. *Let $\hat{x}_{\mathrm{eff}} = x_{\mathrm{eff}}(1)$ and $\hat{x}_{\mathrm{ceff}} = (z_{\mathrm{eff}}(1), 0)^\top$ denote the efficient and constrained-efficient portfolio with unit risk, respectively. Then, the asset demand of the k-th security satisfies*

$$|\langle e_k, \hat{x}_{\mathrm{eff}}\rangle|, |\langle e_k, \hat{x}_{\mathrm{ceff}}\rangle| \leq \langle e_k, V^{-1}e_k\rangle^{\frac{1}{2}}. \tag{A.54}$$

Proof. For every $k \neq n$ the Cauchy-Schwarz inequality implies that

$$\langle e_k, V^{-1}\pi\rangle^2 \leq \langle e_k, V^{-1}e_k\rangle\langle \pi, V^{-1}\pi\rangle$$

[3] STEVENS (1998) also derives an explicit form of the inverse covariance matrix. The entries of this precision matrix are expressed in terms of the regression coefficients and residual variances.

and $\langle e_k, W\pi\rangle^2 \leq \langle e_k, V^{-1}e_k\rangle\langle \pi, W\pi\rangle$ whenever $e_k \neq \alpha\pi$ for all $\alpha \in \mathbb{R}$. □

Hence, Proposition A.2 provides a simple criterion to verify the efficiency of a normalised portfolio with unit risk. Whenever the amount of shares invested to or borrowed from the asset is larger than its reciprocal residual standard deviation, the portfolio mix is neither efficient nor constrained-efficient. For the special case of a diagonal covariance matrix, the term $\langle e_k, V^{-1}e_k\rangle^{\frac{1}{2}}$ corresponds to the inverse standard deviation of asset k's gross return.

A.3 Primitive expectations

This section considers investors who have estimates of non-zero excess returns merely on the regulated asset. These are investors who participate in the financial market with the aim to solely trade asset n. In real life, this assumption is rather an exceptional case. Nevertheless, for the sake of completeness, we will analyse the optimal portfolio selection for this setting as well. It turns out that only value-maximising portfolios are still well-defined. They are mean-variance efficient in the sense of Markowitz with respect to the upper bound of risk $\underline{\sigma}$. However, the uniqueness of a value-maximising portfolio is not guaranteed any more.

Geometrically, the assumption of primitive expectations on value-maximising investors implies that the slope of the short-sale constraint equals to the slope of the objective function. If a value-maximising investor estimates a positive excess return on the regulated asset, she will invest her entire endowment in a long position of the regulated security. Thus, as shown in Figure A.2(a), the short-sale restriction is not binding. Otherwise, if the expectations on the n-th asset are negative, the value-maximising investor would prefer to short-sale asset n such that the constraint gets binding. Figure A.2(b) illustrates that the efficient solutions are not uniquely determined but given by the set $X_{\text{ceff}} := \{x \in \mathbb{R}^n \mid \sigma(x) \leq \sigma \wedge x^{(n)} = \chi\}$. The following proposition formalises this observation.

Proposition A.3 (Value Maximisation). *Let $e_n = \alpha\pi$ for some $\alpha \in \mathbb{R}$. Then the following holds true.*

- *If $\pi^{(n)} > 0$, the short-sale restriction is not binding and the mean-variance efficient portfolio*

$$x_{\text{ceff}}(\sigma, \chi) = x_{\text{eff}}(\sigma)$$

  is the unique solution to (A.1).

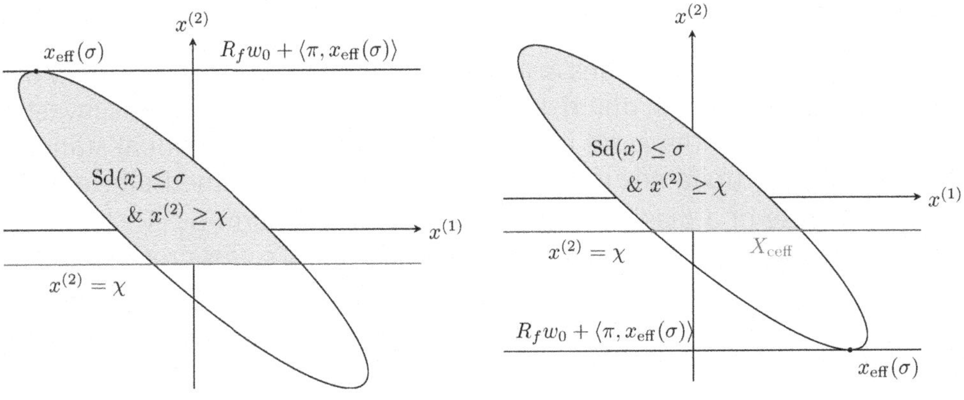

(a) Positive excess return: $\pi^{(2)} > 0$ (b) Negative excess return: $\pi^{(2)} < 0$

Figure A.2: Value-maximising investor with primitive expectations

- *If* $\pi^{(n)} < 0$, *the solution to* (A.1) *is not unique and given by the set*

$$X_{\mathrm{ceff}} := \{x \in \mathbb{R}^n \mid \sigma(x) \leq \sigma \wedge x^{(n)} = \chi\}.$$

In particular, $x_{\mathrm{ceff}}(\underline{\sigma}) \in X_{\mathrm{ceff}}$.

Moreover, if $\pi = 0$ *then* $x_{\mathrm{ceff}} = 0$.

As for the *value-maximising investor*, the short-sale restriction is not binding for the *risk-minimising investor* whenever $\pi^{(n)} > 0$. This is depicted in Figure A.3(a). If $\pi^{(n)} < 0$, the short-sale constraint is binding and the set of feasible portfolios is given by $X = \{x \in \mathbb{R}^n \mid R_f w_0 + \pi^{(n)} x^{(n)} \geq \mu \; \wedge x^{(n)} \geq \chi\}$.[4] It can easily be shown that X is non-empty if and only if the prescribed level of return is smaller than $\underline{\mu} = R_f w_0 + \rho \frac{\chi}{\langle e_n, \hat{x}_{\mathrm{eff}} \rangle}$. Therefore, as illustrated in Figure A.3(b), the constrained-efficient portfolio coincides with the efficient portfolio only if $\mu < \underline{\mu}$. Otherwise no feasible portfolio exists.

Proposition A.4 **(Risk Minimisation).** *Let* $e_n = \alpha \pi$ *for some* $\alpha \in \mathbb{R}$. *Then the following holds true.*

- *If* $\pi^{(n)} > 0$, *the mean-variance efficient portfolio*

$$\hat{x}_{\mathrm{ceff}}(\mu, \chi) = x_{\mathrm{eff}} \left(\frac{\mu - R_f w_0}{\sqrt{\langle \pi, V^{-1} \pi \rangle}} \right)$$

is the unique solution to

$$\min_{x \in X} \mathrm{Sd}(x) \;\; \text{s.t.} \;\; \mathrm{M}(x) \geq \mu. \tag{A.55}$$

[4] Note that, $\langle \pi, x \rangle = \pi^{(n)} x^{(n)}$, as $\pi^{(k)} = 0$ for all $k \neq n$.

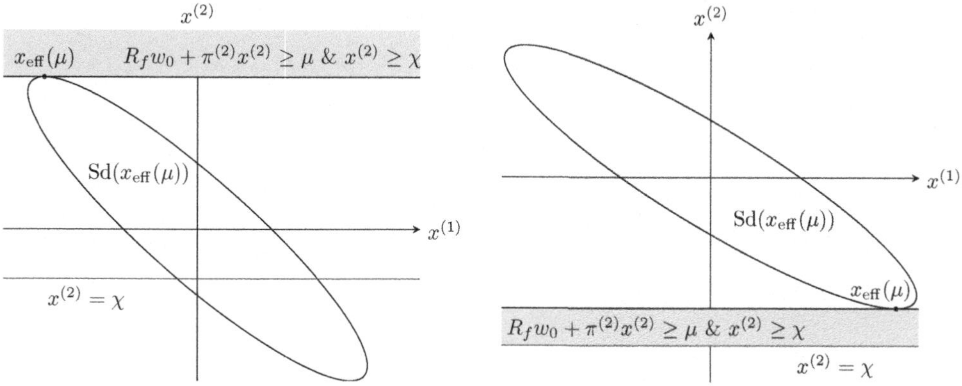

(a) Positive excess return: $\pi^{(2)} > 0$ (b) Negative excess return: $\pi^{(2)} < 0$

Figure A.3: Risk-minimising investor with primitive expectations

- *If* $\pi^{(n)} < 0$, *the solution to* (A.55) *is given by the unconstrained mean-variance efficient portfolio* $x_{\text{eff}}\left(\frac{\mu - R_f w_0}{\sqrt{\langle \pi, V^{-1}\pi \rangle}}\right)$ *whenever* $\mu \leq \underline{\mu}$. *Otherwise, no feasible solution exists.*

Moreover, if $\pi = 0$ *then* $\hat{x}_{\text{ceff}} = 0$.

Proposition A.4 shows that the constrained-efficient portfolio coincides with the efficient portfolio whenever $\mu \leq \underline{\mu}$. Hence, the constrained-efficient frontier coincides with the efficient frontier for $\mu \leq \underline{\mu}$ (or, equivalently, for $\sigma \leq \underline{\sigma}$). If the prescribed level of return is larger than $\underline{\mu}$, the risk-minimising investor is not able to accomplish the prescribed level of return thereby fulfilling the short-sale restriction. The constrained-efficient frontier then collapses to the single point $(\underline{\sigma}, \underline{\mu})$ if $\mu \geq \underline{\mu}$. This is depicted in Figure A.4.

Theorem A.1 (Separation theorem). *Let the hypotheses of Assumptions 1 and 2 be satisfied and assume in addition that* $\sqrt{\langle \pi, V^{-1}\pi \rangle} < \rho_U(R_f w_0)$ *with* $e_n = \alpha\pi$ *for some* $\alpha \in \mathbb{R}$. *Then the optimisation problem* (A.13) *admits a unique solution* $x^* \in \mathbb{R}^n$ *which takes the form of the efficient portfolio* $x_c^* = \sigma^* \hat{x}_{\text{eff}}$, *where*

$$\sigma^* = \underset{\sigma \in [0, \underline{\sigma}]}{\arg\max}\, U(R_f w_0 + \rho\sigma, \sigma). \tag{A.56}$$

Proof. Suppose $\pi^{(k)} = 0$ for all $k \neq n$. Since $S(\underline{\mu}, \underline{\sigma}) < \rho$ was assumed and an optimal solution must be constrained-efficient, the utility maximising portfolio is given by the boundary solution $x^* = x_{\text{ceff}}(\underline{\sigma}, \chi)$.. □

If the investor has primitive expectations, a binding short-sale constraint will force the investor with mean-variance preferences to reduce its optimal level

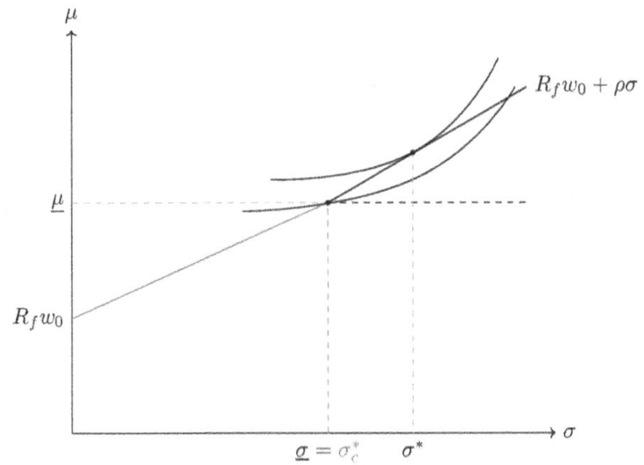

Figure A.4: Separation theorem

of risk to $\underline{\sigma}$ (see Figure A.4). The optimal portfolio x_c^* is then mean-variance efficient in the sense of Markowitz and collinear to $\hat{x}_{\text{eff}}$.

A.4 Slutsky decomposition

In this section we briefly develop the *Slutsky decomposition* for our utility maximisation problem. The decomposition is well-know in microeconomics but takes a slightly unusual form in our context.

Consider the expenditure-minimisation problem of an investor which in our case is given by

$$\min_{\mu,\sigma\geq 0} \mu - \rho\sigma \quad \text{s.t.} \quad U(\mu,\sigma) \geq u_0, \tag{A.57}$$

where u_0 is a prescribed level of utility the investor is seeking for. The solution to (A.57) is given by the income-compensated demand for risk

$$\psi(\rho, u_0) = \arg\max_{\sigma\geq 0} \left\{ I(\sigma, u_0) - \rho\sigma, \ \text{s.t.}\ U(I(\sigma, u_0), \sigma) \geq u_0 \right\},$$

with $I(\sigma, u_0)$ being the indifference curve parametrised in σ.

Proposition A.5 (Slutsky decomposition). *Let the hypotheses of Assumption 1 be satisfied. Then the following holds true.*

1. *For all $(w_0, \rho) \in \mathbb{R}_+^2$,*

$$\frac{\partial\varphi}{\partial\rho}(w_0, \rho) = \frac{\partial\psi}{\partial\rho}(\rho, u_0) + \varphi(w_0, \rho)\frac{\partial\varphi}{\partial w_0}(w_0, \rho), \tag{A.58}$$

where u_0 is a given level of utility.

2. *For each u_0, the compensated demand for risk $\psi(\rho, u_0)$ is increasing in ρ.*[5]

Proof. Let $\psi(\rho, u_0)$ be the income-compensated demand for a given price of risk ρ and the utility level u_0.

1. The duality of the income-compensated demand $\psi(\rho, u_0)$ and the willingness to assume risk $\varphi(\rho, w_0)$ imply

$$\psi(\rho, u_0) = \varphi(\rho, e(\rho, u_0)), \tag{A.59}$$

where $e(\rho, u_0)$ is the expenditure function for given $(\rho, u_0) \in \mathbb{R}^2$. Differentiating both sides of (A.59) yields

$$\frac{\partial \psi(\rho, u_0)}{\partial \rho} = \frac{\partial \varphi(\rho, e(\rho, u_0))}{\partial \rho} + \frac{\partial \varphi(\rho, e(\rho, u_0))}{\partial w_0} \frac{\partial e(\rho, u_0)}{\partial \rho}. \tag{A.60}$$

Shephard's lemma implies that

$$\frac{\partial e(\rho, u_0)}{\partial \rho} = -\psi(\rho, u_0). \tag{A.61}$$

Setting $w_0 = e(\rho, u_0)$ and inserting (A.61) into (A.60) yields

$$\frac{\partial \varphi(\rho, w_0)}{\partial \rho} = \frac{\partial \psi(\rho, u_0)}{\partial \rho} + \varphi(\rho, w_0) \frac{\partial \varphi(\rho, w_0)}{\partial w_0}.$$

2. Since the expenditure function is a convex function of the price of risk ρ, applying Shephard's lemma gives

$$\frac{\partial \psi(\rho, u)}{\partial \rho} = \frac{\partial^2 e(\rho, u)}{\partial^2 \rho} \geq 0,$$

showing that the substitution effect for risk is always non-negative.

□

A.5 Elliptical distributions

This part of the appendix reviews some basic properties of elliptical distributions which play a major role in portfolio theory (see e.g. INGERSOLL (1987)). The reader is referred to the textbooks HÄRDLE AND SIMAR (2012), FANG AND ZHANG (1990) and FANG ET AL. (1990) for proofs and further results.

[5] This corresponds to the well-known microeconomic result that the Hicksian substitution effect is always non-negative.

The class of elliptical distributions, first introduced by KELKER (1970), is a generalisation of normal distributions and shares many of their tractable properties. Let $(\Omega, \mathcal{F}, \mathbb{P})$ be a probability space and denote the Borelian-σ-algebra of the Euclidean space $\mathbb{R}^n$ by $\mathcal{B}(\mathbb{R}^n)$. Recall that the probability distribution ν of a random variable $\tilde{q} : \Omega \to \mathbb{R}^n$ is defined by $\nu_{\tilde{q}}(B) := \mathbb{P}\left(\tilde{q}^{-1}(B)\right)$ for all $B \in \mathcal{B}(\mathbb{R}^n)$. Elliptical distributions are generated by the class of spherical distributions which are defined as follows.

Definition A.1. *A random variable $\tilde{\varepsilon}$ with distribution $\nu_{\tilde{\varepsilon}}$ is said to be* spherically distributed *and $\nu_{\tilde{\varepsilon}}$ is called a* spherical distribution, *if for any orthogonal matrix $\Gamma \in \mathbb{R}^{n\times n}$, it holds that $\tilde{\varepsilon} \overset{\mathcal{D}}{=} \Gamma\tilde{\varepsilon}$, where the relation $\overset{\mathcal{D}}{=}$ indicates that both sides have the same distribution.*

An example of a spherical distribution is the multivariate normal distribution with mean value μ and covariance matrix $\Sigma = \mathbb{1}_n$. Clearly, spherical distributions are invariant under any orthogonal transformation. One of their important properties is characterised in the next theorem.

Theorem A.2.

1. *A random variable $\tilde{\varepsilon} = (\tilde{\varepsilon}^{(n)}, \dots, \tilde{\varepsilon}^{(n)})$ is spherically distributed if and only if $\langle a, \tilde{\varepsilon}\rangle \overset{\mathcal{D}}{=} \|a\|\tilde{\varepsilon}_1$ for any vector $a \in \mathbb{R}^n$. In particular, if $\tilde{\varepsilon}$ is spherically distributed, then $\tilde{\varepsilon}_1$ is spherically distributed as well.*

2. *The first two moments of a spherically distributed random variable $\tilde{\varepsilon}$ satisfy*

$$\mathbb{E}[\tilde{\varepsilon}] = 0 \quad \textit{and} \quad \mathbb{V}[\tilde{\varepsilon}] = \mathbb{E}[\tilde{\varepsilon}^2] = \lambda\mathbb{1}_n$$

   where $\lambda > 0$.

Theorem A.2 establishes a relation between spherical distributions on $\mathbb{R}^n$ and $\mathbb{R}$, stating that all marginal distributions of a spherically distributed random variable are spherical. Moreover, Theorem A.2 ensures that the mean of a spherically distributed random variable is zero and the second moment is a positive multiple of the identity matrix. The class of spherically distributed random variables forms the class of *elliptically distributed* variables by an affine-linear transformation.

Definition A.2. *A random variable $\tilde{q}$ is said to be elliptically distribution, if there exists a spherically distributed random variable $\tilde{\varepsilon}$ and a $n \times n$ matrix A such that $\tilde{q}$ has the same distribution as $\mu + A\tilde{\varepsilon}$, i.e.*

$$\tilde{q} \overset{\mathcal{D}}{=} \mu + A\tilde{\varepsilon}. \tag{A.62}$$

Since spherical distributions are invariant under orthogonal transformations, the representation (A.62) is unique up to orthogonal transformations. An elliptically distributed random variable $\tilde{q}$ may be characterised by a pair (μ, V)

consisting of a vector $\mu \in \mathbb{R}^n$ and a symmetric and positive definite matrix $V \in \mathbb{R}^{n \times n}$.

Corollary A.1. *Let $\tilde{q}$ be an elliptically distributed random variable, i.e. $\tilde{q} \overset{\mathcal{D}}{=} \mu + A\tilde{\varepsilon}$, with values in $\mathbb{R}^n$. Then its first two moments satisfy*

$$\mathbb{E}[\tilde{q}] = \mu \quad \textit{and} \quad \mathbb{V}[\tilde{q}] = V,$$

where $V = AA^\top$.

Corollary A.1 ensures that the distribution $\nu_{\tilde{q}}$ can be associated with the corresponding parameters μ and V, writing $\nu_{\tilde{q}} \equiv \nu_{\mu,V}$. Since V is a positive definite matrix and spherical random variables are invariant with respect to orthogonal transformations, we may without loss of generality set $A := V^{\frac{1}{2}}$, where $V^{\frac{1}{2}}$ denotes the square root of the matrix V (see HILLEBRAND (2008)). Equation (A.62) thus, implies that the spherically distributed random variable $\tilde{\varepsilon}$ generates an elliptical random variable $\tilde{q}$ via an affine-linear transformation

$$e \longmapsto \mu + V^{\frac{1}{2}} e, \quad e \in \mathbb{R}^n.$$

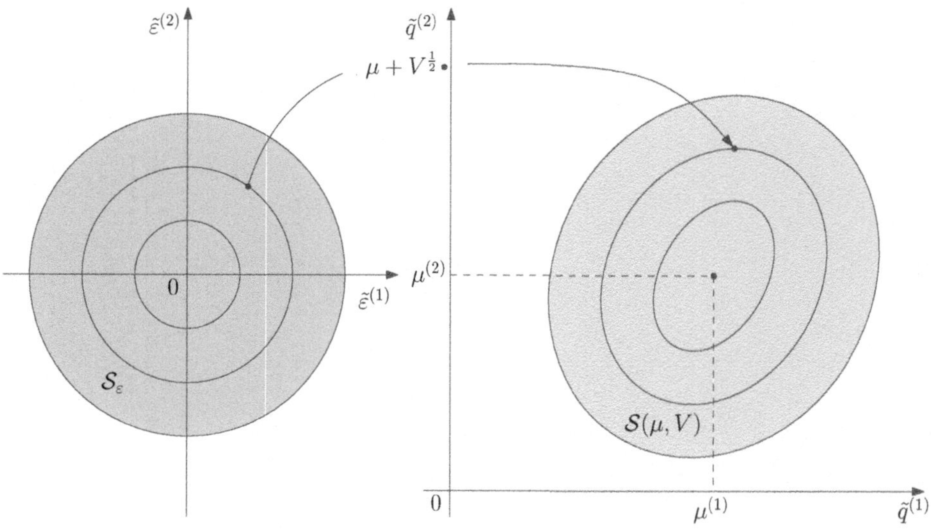

Figure A.5: Affine-linear transformation of $\tilde{q}$ from $\tilde{\varepsilon}$

Denoting by $\mathcal{S}_\varepsilon := \{e \in \mathbb{R}^n \mid \|e\| \leq \bar{\varepsilon}\}$ the *support* of the random variable $\tilde{\varepsilon}$ where $\bar{\varepsilon} > 0$ and $\|\cdot\|$ is the Euclidean norm on $\mathbb{R}^n$, the support of the random variable $\tilde{q}$ becomes

$$\mathcal{S}(\mu, V) := \{\mu + V^{\frac{1}{2}} e \mid e \in \mathcal{S}_\varepsilon\}.$$

Figure A.5 is taken from HILLEBRAND (2008) and illustrates the relation between the random variables $\tilde{\varepsilon}$ and $\tilde{q}$ for the two-asset case.
The most important reason for using the class of elliptically distributed random variables in the theory of portfolio choice is their invariance with respect to affine-linear transformations. This property is formalised in the following corollary.

Corollary A.2. *Let $\tilde{q} \sim \mathcal{E}_n(\mu, V)$ be an elliptically distributed random variable with values in $\mathbb{R}^n$. Then for any matrix $B \in \mathbb{R}^{k \times n}$ with rank $k \leq n$ and any vector $\eta \in \mathbb{R}^k$, the random variable $\tilde{w} := \eta + B\tilde{q}$ satisfies*

$$\tilde{w} \sim \mathcal{E}_k(\eta + B\mu, BVB^\top).$$

Corollary A.2 implies that any linear combination of elliptically distributed random variables are elliptically distributed. Hence, the marginal distributions of elliptically distributed random variables are again elliptical.

Bibliography

Alexander, G. J., "Short selling and efficient sets," *The Journal of Finance* 48 (1993), 1497–1506.

Allingham, M., "Existence theorems in the capital asset pricing model," *Econometrica: Journal of the Econometric Society* (1991), 1169–1174.

Anderson, R. W. and J.-P. Danthine, "Cross hedging," *Journal of Political Economy* 89 (1981), 1182–1196.

Anufriev, M. and J. Tuinstra, "The impact of short-selling constraints on financial market stability in a heterogeneous agents model," *Journal of Economic Dynamics and Control* 37 (2013), 1523–1543.

Asness, C., *Short selling: strategies, risks, and rewards*, volume 137 (John Wiley & Sons, 2004).

BaFin, B., "BaFin Journal 05/10 - Mitteilungen der Bundesanstalt für Finanzdienstleistungen," (2010).

Basak, S. and D. Cuoco, "An equilibrium model with restricted stock market participation," *The Review of Financial Studies* 11 (1998), 309–341.

Black, F., "Capital market equilibrium with restricted borrowing," *The Journal of Business* 45 (1972), 444–455.

Boehme, R. D., B. R. Danielsen and S. M. Sorescu, "Short-sale constraints, differences of opinion, and overvaluation," *Journal of Financial and Quantitative Analysis* 41 (2006), 455–487.

Böhm, V. and C. Chiarella, "Mean variance preferences, expectations formation, and the dynamics of random asset prices," *Mathematical Finance* 15 (2005), 61–97.

Bongini, L., M. Degli Esposti, C. Giardina and A. Schianchi, "Portfolio optimization with short-selling and spin-glass," *The European Physical Journal B-Condensed Matter and Complex Systems* 27 (2002), 263–272.

G. Hunanyan, *The Consequences of Short-Sale Constraints on the Stability of Financial Markets*, Finanzwirtschaft, Banken und Bankmanagement | Finance, Banks and Bank Management, https://doi.org/10.1007/978-3-658-27956-1

BRIS, A., W. N. GOETZMANN AND N. ZHU, "Efficiency and the bear: Short sales and markets around the world," *The Journal of Finance* 62 (2007), 1029–1079.

CAMBINI, A. AND L. MARTEIN, *Convex Functions* (Springer, 2009).

CHABAKAURI, G., "Dynamic equilibrium with two stocks, heterogeneous investors, and portfolio constraints," *The review of financial studies* 26 (2013), 3104–3141.

CHANCELLOR, E., "A short history of the bear," *Fortune, October* (2001).

CHANG, E., Y. BAI AND J. WANG, "Asset prices under short-sales constraints," in *Mitsui Life Symposium on Financial Markets* (MITSUI LIFE-Financial Research Center, 2006), 43.

CHAROENROOK, A. AND H. DAOUK, "A Study of Market-Wide Short-Selling Restrictions," Working Papers 51180, Cornell University, Department of Applied Economics and Management, June 2009.

CHOIE, K. S. N. AND S. J. HWANG, "Profitability of Short-Selling and Exploitability of Short Information," *The Journal of Portfolio Management, Winter* (1994).

DANA, R., "Existence, Uniqueness and Determinacy of Equilibrium in C.A.P.M. with a Riskless Asset," *Journal of Mathematical Economics* 32 (1999), 167–175.

DANA, R. A., "Existence and uniqueness of equilibria when preferences are additively separable," *Econometrica* 61 (1993), 953–957.

DERCOLE, F. AND D. RADI, "Does the "uptick rule" stabilize the stock market? Insights from Adaptive Rational Equilibrium Dynamics," *arXiv preprint arXiv:1405.7747* (2014).

DIAMOND, D. W. AND R. E. VERRECCHIA, "Constraints on short-selling and asset price adjustment to private information," *Journal of Financial Economics* 18 (1987), 277–311.

DYBVIG, P. H., "Short sales restrictions and kinks on the mean variance frontier," *The Journal of Finance* 39 (1984), 239–244.

FAMA, E. F. AND K. R. FRENCH, "The capital asset pricing model: Theory and evidence," *The Journal of Economic Perspectives* 18 (2004), 25–46.

FANG, K. AND Y. ZHANG, "Generalized Multivariate Analysis. 1990," (1990).

FANG, K.-T., S. KOTZ AND K. W. NG, *Symmetric multivariate and related distributions* (Chapman and Hall, 1990).

FELLNER, G. AND E. THEISSEN, "Short sale constraints, divergence of opinion and asset prices: Evidence from the laboratory," *Journal of Economic Behavior & Organization* 101 (2014), 113–127.

FIGLEWSKI, S., "The informational effects of restrictions on short sales: Some empirical evidence," *Journal of Financial and Quantitative Analysis* 16 (1981), 463–476.

FIGLEWSKI, S. AND G. P. WEBB, "Options, short sales, and market completeness," *The Journal of Finance* 48 (1993), 761–777.

GALLMEYER, M. AND B. HOLLIFIELD, "An examination of heterogeneous beliefs with a short-sale constraint in a dynamic economy," *Review of Finance* 12 (2008), 323–364.

GREGORIOU, G. N., *Handbook of short selling* (Academic Press, 2011).

GRUBE, R. C. AND W. L. BEEDLES, "Effects of short-sale restrictions," *Journal of Business Research* 9 (1981), 231–236.

GULEN, H. AND S. MAYHEW, "Stock index futures trading and volatility in international equity markets," *Journal of Futures Markets: Futures, Options, and Other Derivative Products* 20 (2000), 661–685.

HÄRDLE, W. AND L. SIMAR, *Applied Multivariate Statistical Analysis* (Springer, 2012).

HARRISON, J. M. AND D. M. KREPS, "Speculative investor behavior in a stock market with heterogeneous expectations," *The Quarterly Journal of Economics* 92 (1978), 323–336.

HARUVY, E. AND C. N. NOUSSAIR, "The effect of short selling on bubbles and crashes in experimental spot asset markets," *The Journal of Finance* 61 (2006), 1119–1157.

HENS, T., J. LAITENBERGER AND A. LÖFFLER, "Two remarks on the uniqueness of equilibria in the CAPM," *Journal of Mathematical Economics* 37 (2002), 123–132.

HENS, T. AND K. R. SCHENK-HOPPÉ, *Handbook of financial markets: dynamics and evolution* (Elsevier, 2009).

HILLEBRAND, M., *Pension systems, demographic change, and the stock market*, volume 610 (Springer, 2008).

HO, K. W., "Short-sales restrictions and volatility The case of the Stock Exchange of Singapore," *Pacific-Basin Finance Journal* 4 (1996), 377–391.

HUNANYAN, G. AND J. WENZELBURGER, "On the Effectiveness of Capital Requirements," Working paper, 2018a.

———, "On the Reduction of Default Risk of Financial Intermediaries," Working paper, 2018b.

INGERSOLL, J. E., *Theory of financial decision making*, volume 3 (Rowman & Littlefield, 1987).

JARROW, R., "Heterogeneous expectations, restrictions on short sales, and equilibrium asset prices," *The Journal of Finance* 35 (1980), 1105–1113.

JONES, C. M. AND O. A. LAMONT, "Short-sale constraints and stock returns," *Journal of Financial Economics* 66 (2002), 207–239.

KELKER, D., "Distribution theory of spherical distributions and a location-scale parameter generalization," *Sankhyā: The Indian Journal of Statistics, Series A* (1970), 419–430.

KOCH-MEDINA, P. AND J. WENZELBURGER, "Equilibria in the CAPM with non-tradeable endowments," *Journal of Mathematical Economics* 75 (2018), 93 – 107.

KOGAN, L., I. MAKAROV AND R. UPPAL, "The equity risk premium and the riskfree rate in an economy with borrowing constraints," *Mathematics and Financial Economics* 1 (2007), 1–19.

KRAUS, A. AND A. RUBIN, "The effect of short sale constraint removal on volatility in the presence of heterogeneous beliefs," *International Review of Finance* 4 (2003), 171–188.

LEVY, H., "The capital asset pricing model: Theory and empiricism," *The Economic Journal* 93 (1983), 145–165.

LEVY, H. AND M. SARNAT, *Capital investment and financial decisions* (Pearson Education, 1994).

LEVY, M., "Measuring Portfolio Performance: Sharpe, Alpha, or the Geometric Mean?," *Journal of Investment Management* 15 (2017), 1–17.

LEVY, M. AND Y. RITOV, "Mean-variance efficient portfolios with many assets: 50% short," *Quantitative Finance* 11 (2011), 1461–1471.

LINTNER, J., "The Valuation of Risk Assets and the Selection of Risky Investments in Stock Portfolios and Capital Budgets," *The Review of Economics and Statistics* 47 (1965), 13–37.

———, "The Aggregation of Investor's Diverse Judgments and Preferences in Purely Competitive Security Markets," *Journal of Financial and Quantitative Analysis* 4 (1969), 347–400.

LIU, H. AND Y. WANG, "Asset pricing implications of short-sale constraints in imperfectly competitive markets," *Management Science* (2018).

MARKOWITZ, H. M., "Portfolio Selection," *The Journal of Finance* 7 (1952), 77–91.

———, "Risk adjustment," *Journal of Accounting, Auditing & Finance* 5 (1990), 213–225.

MILLER, E. M., "Risk, uncertainty, and divergence of opinion," *The Journal of finance* 32 (1977), 1151–1168.

MISRA, V., M. LAGI AND Y. BAR-YAM, "Evidence of market manipulation in the financial crisis," *arXiv preprint arXiv:1112.3095* (2011).

MOSSIN, J., "Equilibrium in a Capital Asset Market," *Econometrica* (1966).

NAGEL, S., "Short sales, institutional investors and the cross-section of stock returns," *Journal of financial economics* 78 (2005), 277–309.

NAKATA, H., "Welfare effects of short-sale constraints under heterogeneous beliefs," *Economic Theory* 53 (2013), 283–314.

NIELSEN, L. T., "Uniqueness of equilibrium in the classical capital asset pricing model," *Journal of Financial and Quantitative Analysis* 23 (1988), 329–336.

———, "Equilibrium in CAPM without a riskless asset," *The Review of Economic Studies* 57 (1990a), 315–324.

———, "Existence of equilibrium in CAPM," *Journal of Economic Theory* 52 (1990b), 223–231.

ROCHET, J., "Capital requirements and the behaviour of commercial banks," *European Economic Review* 36 (1992), 1137–1170.

ROLL, R., "A critique of the asset pricing theory's tests Part I: On past and potential testability of the theory," *Journal of financial economics* 4 (1977), 129–176.

ROSS, S. A., "The Capital Asset Pricing Model (CAPM), Short-Sale Restrictions and Related Issues," *Journal of Finance* 32 (1977), 177–83.

SAFFI, P. A. AND K. SIGURDSSON, "Price efficiency and short selling," *The Review of Financial Studies* 24 (2010), 821–852.

SCHILLING, N. AND J. WENZELBURGER, "Simtools Manual," (2018).

SCHNABEL, J. A., "Short sales restrictions and the security market line," *Journal of Business Research* 12 (1984), 87–96.

SHARPE, W. F., "Capital asset prices: A theory of market equilibrium under conditions of risk," *The journal of finance* 19 (1964), 425–442.

SMIMOU, K., C. BECTOR AND G. JACOBY, "Portfolio selection subject to experts' judgments," *International Review of Financial Analysis* 17 (2008), 1036–1054.

SPANAUS, C., *Economics of Downside Risk*, Ph.D. thesis, Technische Universität Kaiserslautern, Fachbereich Wirtschaftswissenschaften (2018).

STEVENS, G. V., "On the inverse of the covariance matrix in portfolio analysis," *The Journal of Finance* 53 (1998), 1821–1827.

TOBIN, J., "Liquidity preference as behavior towards risk," *Oxford Univ. Press* 25 (1958), 65–86.

WENZELBURGER, J., "Learning to predict rationally when beliefs are heterogeneous," *Journal of Economic Dynamics and Control* 28 (2004), 2075–2104.

———, "Perfect forecasting, behavioral heterogeneities, and asset prices," *Handbook of Financial Markets: Dynamics and Evolution, Handbooks in Finance* (2009), 345–401.

———, "The two-fund separation theorem revisited," *Annals of Finance* 6 (2010), 221–239.

———, "Economics of Banking," (2018a).

———, "On the Notion of a Modified Market Portfolio," *Available at SSRN 2845968* (2018b).

WON, D., G. HAHN AND N. YANNELIS, "Capital market equilibrium without riskless assets: heterogeneous expectations," *Annals of Finance* 4 (2008), 183–195.

XIONG, W., "Bubbles, crises, and heterogeneous beliefs," Technical Report, National Bureau of Economic Research, 2013.

ZHANG, H. H., "Endogenous short-sale constraint, stock prices and output cycles," *Macroeconomic Dynamics* 1 (1997), 228–254.

The manufacturer's authorised representative in the EU is Springer Nature Customer Service Centre GmbH, Europaplatz 3, 69115 Heidelberg, Germany. If you have any concerns regarding our products, please contact ProductSafety@springernature.com

Printed and bound by CPI Group (UK) Ltd, Croydon, CR0 4YY
30/09/2026
02225576-0015